COUNTRY LIVING

COUNTRY
COOK

COUNTRY LIVING

COUNTRY COOK

PHILIPPA DAVENPORT

EBURY PRESS
LONDON

NOTE ON MEASUREMENTS

The recipes in this book were written and tested by the
author in imperial and metric. American measures have
been included by the publishers.
Strictly speaking, 1 imperial tablespoon equals $1\frac{1}{2}$ American
tablespoons, but for the small quantities used in this book
it is not necessary to adjust measurements.

Published by Ebury Press
Division of The National Magazine Company Ltd
Colquhoun House
27–37 Broadwick Street
London W1V 1FR

First impression 1987

COUNTRY COOK was first published as monthly articles in
COUNTRY LIVING magazine between 1985 and 1987

ISBN 0 85223 665 4

Edited by Veronica Sperling
Art Direction by Frank Phillips
Design by Bill Mason

Filmset by Advanced Filmsetters (Glasgow) Ltd
Printed and bound in Italy by New Interlitho, S.p.a., Milan

CONTENTS

INTRODUCTION

Writing for Country Living seems a natural extension of life in and around my kitchen because I have been encouraged to record my thoughts and experiences of cooking for family and friends as the months go by. The result is a celebration of the passing seasons—for seasonality is the greedy inspiration on which my cooking depends.

What is freshest and best in the garden, fields and shops is what I want for the cooking pot. When herbs tumble thickly over the kitchen path, when trout dart and rise for mayfly, when the hens start to lay extra eggs, when the hedgerows become a tangle of blackberries, or when our supermarket is scented with Sevilles, then I know it is time to cook and eat these foods.

Our menus too are a reflection of changing moods in the weather. When the sun beats down I want little more than the delicate bite of crisp salad leaves, cool green herbs and juicy scarlet fruits. When there is a frosty nip in the air my thoughts instinctively turn to good honest stews and pies, and to soups as thick and warm as Shetland pullovers.

LEFT TO RIGHT: GREEN TEA CREAMS (PAGE 15), FLOATING ISLANDS (PAGE 15)

My recipes are fairly simple. I don't have the time or inclination to spend hours fussing over the stove. What is more, I am convinced that elaboration is usually self-defeating. If the ingredients are the freshest and best of their kind—whether they be humble cabbage or glorious grouse—simple good cooking will show them off to maximum advantage. Some of my dishes are traditional, some are new. I have delved into the past, sometimes adapting old recipes to suit today's tastes; I have drawn on my imagination; and I have gleaned tips from friends and neighbours both here in England and when I lived abroad.

I use plenty of fresh vegetables and fruits; the emphasis on red meats is slight. This is in line with current nutritional advice but it is nothing new. Country cooks all over the world have known for centuries that to use locally grown vegetables and cereals in abundance, to eke out hard-won cultivated crops with foods gathered freely from the wild, and to use meat and fish sparingly, are the best ways to enjoy tasty and nutritious meals while carefully husbanding the resources of the land.

Philippa Davenport

MARCH 1987

PHILIPPA DAVENPORT
WHITTONDITCH

For Jane,
with special affection

SPRING

Spring begins for me with the cracking of Easter eggs. It is the season of hope and wonderful energy as grasses grow lush, buds break into blossom and vegetable seedlings grow strong.

Fresh from the Dairy

The month of May has always been a very busy time for dairy maids. In fact, it used to be called "Thrimilce", meaning that cows could be milked three times a day.

Traditionally, the foaming fresh milk was cooled and skimmed in large shallow pans. Some was then scalded and clotted to a golden crusted cream, some was hand-churned to produce butter and buttermilk, and any surplus was used for making into cheese. Usually, both butter and cheese were heavily salted, which was necessary to prolong keeping quality in the days before refrigeration. Even so, they say you could tell which farm dairy produce came from because of the flavour of the local wild flowers.

Today milk is still regarded as the most complete food, and it is acknowledged to be supremely versatile in cooking. Butter, cream and hard cheese will always be vital ingredients in good country cooking, but the emphasis is changing as cooks discover the pleasures of making and eating lighter dairy products.

No cook worth her salt would dream of dismissing from her repertoire such classic treats as traditional trifle, old-fashioned syllabubs and home-made ice creams. But those who care about good health, as well as good eating, are learning to temper indulgence. Such dishes are sensibly reserved for very special occasions. Other simpler and less rich traditional recipes are being revived, and exciting new alternatives are beginning to emerge.

Few people now make their own butter and cream, but increasing numbers take pride in producing home-made yoghurt and fresh soft cheeses. There is something particularly appealing about these foods. They are deliciously creamy yet clean-tasting and light—a joy to eat as they are, and equally valuable in cooking.

FRESH HOME-MADE YOGHURT
This is wonderfully different from the thin acidic commercial varieties, and is particularly good when made from fresh full-cream milk which has been reduced by simmering.

Good yoghurt can, for example, be eaten with a little orange juice and honey to make a splendid slimline alternative to pouring cream. It can be whizzed in a blender with fresh herbs and tomatoes or cucumber to make cool summery soups, and it can be used in marinades to tenderise and subtly flavour poultry and meats.

Just one word of warning: yoghurt won't work if the milk is too hot or too cold. Dipping a finger into the milk pan, or hoping the airing cupboard is warm enough, is too vague. For perfect results every time use a thermometer and incubate the yoghurt in an insulated plastic picnic jar.

To make 1 pint/2½ cups (575 ml) yoghurt, first simmer 1½ pints/3¾ cups (850 ml) silver-top or gold-top milk until reduced by one third and set aside until cooled to 120°F (49°C). Rinse out with warm water a wide-mouthed insulated jar of 1 pint/2½ cups (575 ml) capacity. Put into the jar 1 heaped tsp plain, unpasteurised yoghurt (either shop-bought or saved from the last batch you made). Carefully blend in a few spoonfuls of the prepared milk, then pour on the remaining warm milk and stir to mix thoroughly. Cover the jar with its lid and leave undisturbed for about 5 hours until the yoghurt has set.

Transfer the covered jar to the fridge and chill the yoghurt for about 3 hours before using. Home-made yoghurt will keep for 5–7 days but develops acidity with keeping.

STABILISED YOGHURT
Yoghurt can be used to fine effect in place of some or all of the cream often used in hot sauces, quiches, special casseroles and so on. But unless yoghurt is stabilised, it tends to separate when subjected to high or prolonged heat which spoils the looks of finished dishes.

To stabilise yoghurt, put a little cornflour (1 tsp cornflour per ½ pint/1¼ cups/275 ml yoghurt) into a saucepan and gradually blend in the yoghurt. Place over low heat and stir continuously, in one direction only, until boiling point is reached. Use it at once, or cool, cover and refrigerate until required: it will keep for several days in the refrigerator.

THICKENED YOGHURT
Good yoghurt can help cut the cost (and the sometimes over-rich quality) of desserts and savoury mousses which traditionally include lashings of cream. For healthier and more sophisticated dishes, use yoghurt—alone, or folded into whisked egg whites, or mixed half and half with whipped cream. Thickened yoghurt is usually best for these purposes as it has good "body". To make it, put fresh well chilled yoghurt into a large, double-thick square of buttermuslin, tie with string, hang up and leave for 2–4 hours to drain off some of the moisture.

YOGHURT CHEESE (ALSO CALLED DRY YOGHURT)

The longer buttermuslin-wrapped yoghurt is left to drain, the more moisture it loses. After dripping for 24 hours, it attains the consistency of soft fresh cheese. A delicious addition to the cheeseboard, yoghurt cheese can also be used instead of cottage, curd or cream cheese in such things as stuffed pancakes and pasta dishes, cheesecakes and smoked fish pâtés.

WEST COUNTRY CREAMS

Rich, yet fresh tasting because of the yoghurt, this is a delightful alternative to the usual dish of strawberries and cream. Originally buttermilk or soured cream was used instead of yoghurt, and cottagers who only grew rhubarb and gooseberries in their gardens used stiff purées of these fruits in place of strawberries; in autumn they used blackberries gathered from the hedgerows.

1 lb (450 g) strawberries
a little caster (superfine) sugar
½ pint/1¼ cups (275 ml) yoghurt
½ pint/1¼ cups (275 ml) double (heavy) cream
honey or pale muscovado sugar
ratafias to garnish

Toss the berries in the merest whisper of caster sugar and divide between small dishes or glasses.

Gradually stir the cream into half the yoghurt. Whip the mixture, then fold in the rest of the yoghurt. Spoon the creamy concoction over the fruit and spoon a little honey or brown sugar on top.

Chill the puddings for at least 2 hours (preferably 8 hours) so that the sweetener begins to seep into the cream, and scatter with ratafias just before serving if wished.
SERVES 8

JUMPING JACKS

The French verb for the fast frying of foods in a little very hot fat is "sauter". Literally translated into English this means "to jump", which perhaps explains the name of this excellent little supper dish.

1 lb (450 g) chicken livers
¾ lb (350 g) onions
2¼ oz/generous ½ stick (65 g) unsalted butter
6 fl oz/¾ cup (175 ml) each stabilised yoghurt and soured cream
1 tsp each English mustard and Worcestershire sauce, or more to taste
salt and freshly ground black pepper
half a cup of fresh chopped parsley

Trim the chicken livers and cut them into bite-size pieces. Halve and slice the onions very thinly.

Beat the stabilised yoghurt and soured cream together with the mustard, Worcestershire sauce and plenty of salt and pepper.

Melt most of the butter in a sauté pan and cook the onions very gently until tender. Remove and keep hot. Increase the heat and add the remaining butter. When sizzling hot, add the chicken livers and sauté them for 3 minutes only, until brown and crusted but still tender and pink within.

Quickly pour on the yoghurt mixture. As soon as it bubbles up, return the onions to the pan. Cook, stirring and turning for a few minutes until the sauce is thoroughly hot, slightly thickened and coating the ingredients nicely. Stir in the parsley and serve straight away on a bed of rice or spinach.
SERVES 4–5

CLOCKWISE FROM LEFT: INDIVIDUAL FLOATING ISLANDS, WEST COUNTRY CREAMS (PAGE 13), GREEN TEA CREAMS, ROSE PETAL JUNKET

ROSE PETAL JUNKET

Although its cool simplicity is often greeted as a novelty today, junket (or curds and whey) is an ancient dish. It was traditionally made in the milking parlour, using milk which was foaming and warm straight from the cow, and might be flavoured in a variety of ways. This spectacular version was a speciality of Bath in the 18th century.

1½ pints/3¾ cups (850 ml) creamy milk
1 well heaped tbsp caster (superfine) sugar
1½ tsp liquid junket rennet or
    1½ plain junket tablets
4 tbsp triple distilled rose water
8 fl oz/1 cup (225 ml) whipped or clotted cream, or
    thickened yoghurt
damask rose petals to garnish

Gently warm the milk and sugar to 98°F (37°C). Away from the heat, quickly stir in the liquid rennet (or the finely powdered junket tablets), then the rose water.

Pour the delicately flavoured milk into a pretty dish or individual glasses and leave at room temperature until softly set—about 3 hours if using liquid rennet, ½ hour if using junket tablets.

Just before serving, take the rose petals (from old-fashioned, sweetly scented damask roses if you have some in the garden) and remove the white base tips. Spoon the cream or yoghurt over the junket and scatter with the petals, or with varak (edible silver) or fresh raspberries if old-fashioned roses are unavailable.

SERVES 6–8

GREEN TEA CREAM

In the 17th and 18th centuries, before Indian tea became predominant, green or unfermented tea from China enjoyed considerable success in British drawing-rooms—and at the dinner table, where it was used to flavour delicate desserts such as this.

¾ pint/1⅞ cups (425 ml) creamy milk
¼ oz/1½ tsp (7 g) green (hyson or gunpowder) tea
scant 2 tsp caster (superfine) sugar
1½ tsp gelatine powder
¼ pint/⅔ cup (150 ml) single (light) cream
pistachio nuts or pumpkin seeds to garnish

Scald the milk. Pour it on the tea leaves and sugar, and leave to infuse briefly.

Dissolve the gelatine in 2 tbsp water. Strain the tea, blend in the liquid gelatine and stir in the cream. The characteristic fresh vegetation taste of green tea should be subtly and deliciously evident—if too strong, stir in a little more cream.

Pour the mixture into glasses. Leave in a cool place for about 3 hours until set to a very soft jelly, and garnish with damp tea leaves, a few pistachio nuts or pumpkin seeds just before serving.

If preferred, tea cream can be made in a pretty jelly mould, in which case use twice as much gelatine powder or the cream will collapse when unmoulded.

SERVES 4–5

FLOATING ISLANDS

This long-standing country house favourite is probably the most elegant of all custards. Garnished with early strawberries freshly picked from the garden, it is a splendid dish with which to celebrate the beginning of the soft fruit season.

For the custard:
4 large egg yolks
2 oz/scant ¼ cup (50 g) caster (superfine) sugar
½ tsp cornflour
scant 18 fl oz/2¼ cups (500 ml) hot creamy milk
3 tbsp white rum or triple distilled orange flower water
strawberries or toasted almonds to garnish

For the meringues:
4 large egg whites
2 oz/scant ¼ cup (50 g) caster sugar

Cream the egg yolks in the top part of a double-boiler. Add the sugar and cornflour and beat for a few seconds more. Pour on the hot milk, beating the egg mixture all the time as you pour.

Place the pan over barely simmering water and cook, stirring continuously, until the custard thickens to the consistency of double cream. Turn the custard into a shallow dish or individual glasses and cool slightly before stirring in the flavouring.

Whisk the egg whites until stiff, gradually beating in the sugar. Three-quarters fill a sauté pan with water and bring just below simmering point. Add dessertspoonfuls of the meringue mixture, a few at a time and spaced well apart, and poach very gently for 5 minutes, flipping them over halfway through this time. Drain well on plenty of kitchen paper.

Shortly before serving, pile the meringues on top of the cold custard and garnish with strawberries or toasted almonds.

SERVES 6–8

SPRING CLEAN SOUP

Thrifty country cooks have always eked out their hard-won crops with foods harvested freely from hedgerow and field, and early versions of this soup used mixtures of sorrel, watercress and nettles all gathered from the wild. My version uses garden sorrel and spinach. If you have no sorrel, use a double quantity of spinach and add the juice of 1–2 lemons to give the soup its characteristically refreshing tang. Excellent served hot or cold.

½ lb (225 g) garden or French sorrel
½ lb (225 g) young spinach
1 lb (450 g) potatoes
a bunch of spring onions (scallions)
2½ pints/6¼ cups (1.4 litres) good stock
½ pint/1¼ cups (275 ml) buttermilk
¼ pint/⅔ cup (150 ml) stabilised yoghurt
croûtons or bacon to garnish

Wash the sorrel and spinach, discarding tough stalks. Shake dry and chop finely, using a food processor if possible for the sake of speed.

Peel the potatoes and cut them into small dice. Trim and slice the spring onions in green parts as well as white.

Cook the potatoes and spring onions in the stock for about 7 minutes until nearly tender. Add the sorrel and spinach and simmer for a few minutes more. Add the buttermilk and stabilised yoghurt and bring back to simmering point, stirring all the while.

Season and thin with extra stock or water to taste, and serve garnished with croûtons or snippets of crisp bacon if liked.

SERVES 6–8

SHEPHERD'S SURPRISE

A wholesome country dish using meat, herbs and vegetables at their freshest and best in summer. It is topped with a rather special yoghurt and cheese crust.

1 lb (450 g) lean minced (ground) lamb
1 tbsp olive or peanut oil
1 onion and 1 garlic clove
¾ lb (350 g) tomatoes
salt and freshly ground black pepper
lemon juice and a bunch of mint
1 lb (450 g) French or runner beans

For the topping:
1 oz/heaped ¼ cup (25 g) plain (all-purpose) flour
½ pint/1¼ cups (275 ml) yoghurt
2 eggs

2½ oz/generous ½ cup (65 g) grated Farmhouse Cheddar cheese
freshly ground black pepper

Fry first the meat, then the chopped onion in the oil until nicely browned. Stir in the crushed garlic and the skinned and finely chopped tomatoes, and leave to cook gently for about 20 minutes, just stirring occasionally. If the pan becomes dry, add a little water. If the mixture is too sloppy, increase heat to drive off excess moisture. Season generously with salt and pepper. Add a little lemon juice and plenty of fresh chopped mint, then turn the mixture into a shallow baking dish.

Steam the beans until barely tender (they will continue to cook in the oven) and lay them neatly over the meat.

Beat the yoghurt into the flour with a balloon whisk (because flour is used in this way there is no need to use stabilised yoghurt for this recipe). Add the lightly beaten eggs, the grated cheese and plenty of pepper, and continue beating until smoothly blended.

Spread the topping evenly over the vegetables, and bake for about 45 minutes at 375°F (190°C), mark 5, until the topping is golden and puffy.

SERVES 4

FRESH HERB CHEESE

Pretty and delicious, this is very easy and inexpensive to make. When fresh herbs are not available, spices can replace them: a mixture of toasted sesame, coriander and cumin seeds is particularly good.

¼ lb (125 g) yoghurt cheese
¼ lb (125 g) curd cheese
salt
1 small garlic clove (optional)
fresh parsley and chives, or fresh thyme and marjoram

Mash the cheeses with a fork in a soup plate until smoothly blended. Season lightly with salt, and the crushed garlic if wished. Add 4–5 tbsp of your chosen fresh chopped herbs and mash and mix everything well.

Scoop up the mixture, roll it into a firm ball with your hands, then flatten it into a cake shape. Press more of your chosen herbs all over the surface of the cheese to coat it prettily.

Put the cheese on to a plate lined with a double thickness of kitchen paper, cover it with an upturned bowl and leave in a cool place for a few hours to allow the flavours to blend and infuse.

COOK'S NOTEBOOK

There are 25 souls in the hamlet where I live: there used to be a smithy by the ford, but no longer. We have no pub, no church, no school and no corner shop. Shopping involves trekking a fair number of miles in all directions; farm eggs to the north, best delicatessen to the south, fishmonger to the east and butcher to the west.

Sometimes when the roads are treacherous, or when I've driven 18 frustrating miles in search of something as ordinary as lemons, I'm jealous of those who live in a major town or city. I envy them having a cheesemonger, wine merchant and other specialist shops more or less on the doorstep, not to mention a supermarket open all hours, seven days a week. On the other hand, I am grateful for the lack of traffic wardens and I would not forgo the country privilege of being able to enjoy beautifully fresh home-grown foods for all the tea in China.

Even if you are no gardener yourself, you can usually get most of the vegetables you need, and some fruits, far fresher than you could in a town, by buying from a pick-your-own farm or from the garden gate stalls of cottages.

Down country lanes little wider than the aisles of a posh supermarket you may sometimes find other foods for sale or barter. I buy honey-in-the-comb from a beekeeper whose workers, I imagine, may have sipped nectar from flowers in our garden. I swap my quince jelly and bunches of herbs for creamy milk and soft fresh cheeses made by a goat-keeping neighbour, and I buy fresh free-range eggs from a farmer's wife who still earns "pin money" in this traditional way. Occasionally, a hen whose useful egg-laying days are over may be bought for the pot. Farmers' wives traditionally stew such a bird to tenderise the tough but well-flavoured meat. *Henny Penny* is an adaptation of this sort of good honest country chicken stew, which I have devised for cooking more easily obtainable boiling or roasting chicken—a bird which does need more flavour-boosting but somewhat less cooking time, of course.

Divide a chicken into 4–6 pieces (or buy 4–6 large chicken joints), dust with well seasoned flour and brown in a little fat. Then lightly colour 4 onions cut into quarters, 3 celery stalks sliced into thick crescents, 4 sliced carrots and $\frac{1}{4}$ lb (125 g) streaky bacon rashers (slices) cut into snippets. Put the chicken on top of the vegetables in a casserole. Add the bacon rinds, a long thin spiral of orange peel and a bay leaf (all tied-up in buttermuslin). Pour on $\frac{1}{2}$ pint/ $1\frac{1}{4}$ cups (275 ml) cider to which you have added 1 chicken stock cube, a good grinding of pepper, a little salt and about 1 tsp dried tarragon. Lay a sheet of lightly oiled greaseproof paper directly on top of the ingredients. Cover with a well fitting lid and cook slowly at 300°F (150°C), mark 2 for 2 hours or more until the chicken pieces and all the vegetables are very tender and fragrant.

I love the market. It's such a wonderful mixture and full of surprises. What with one thing and another, a shopping expedition can take hours, and in my experience one can often arrive home badly in need of a good meal but too tired to cook one. The solution, I've discovered, is to do what wise country cooks have always done on market day—prepared a meal before going out.

A dish like *Market Day Beef* is simple to prepare: just assemble the raw ingredients, pile them into a dish, and pop it in the oven so it will cook while you are out and you will be welcomed home by the scent of a delicious hot meal. Mix together about $1\frac{1}{4}$ lb (600 g) braising or stewing beef and half that amount of ox kidney (both cut into chunks), a scant $\frac{1}{2}$ lb/generous $1\frac{1}{2}$ cups (200 g) finely chopped onions, and 4 or more tbsp parsley. Pile them into a casserole that has been greased with dripping. Mix together a good shake each of Worcester sauce and mushroom ketchup, $\frac{1}{2}$ tbsp lemon juice, 2 tsp mustard, a good seasoning of salt and pepper, and enough cold water to make $\frac{1}{2}$ pint/ $1\frac{1}{4}$ cups (275 ml) in total. Pour over the meats, add a bay leaf and press everything down into the dish. Peel and very thinly slice plenty of potatoes overlapping on top of the meat. Season generously between layers, and cover the top layer of potatoes with a thin smear of beef dripping. Do not cover. Cook at 275–300°F (140–150°C), mark 1–2 until the top layer of potatoes become crunchy and the potato and meats underneath become deliciously tender. I find it takes a minimum of 3 hours, 4 hours is usually better and it is the sort of dish which doesn't seem to come to any harm if left for longer. This means there is no need to hurry home.

CUCUMBER CHICKEN WITH TARRAGON CREAM SAUCE

Simple yet sophisticated, this succulent chicken salad with its subtle hint of tarragon owes its inspiration to that great cookery writer of the early 19th century, Eliza Acton.

2 cucumbers
1 tsp salt
2 tsp caster (superfine) sugar
1 tbsp tarragon vinegar
1 cos (romaine) lettuce
4–6 oz/1 cup (125–175 g) peas, shelled weight
1 × 3¼–4 lb (1.6–1.8 kg) poached chicken

For the sauce:
7½ fl oz/scant 1 cup (215 ml) each yoghurt and
    mayonnaise
3 tbsp good chicken stock
fresh tarragon sprigs

Peel, halve and seed the cucumbers. Cut the flesh into matchstick-size pieces. Put them into a bowl. Add the salt, sugar and vinegar. Toss gently and leave for 45 minutes before draining and patting dry.

Carefully beat the yoghurt into the mayonnaise. Add the cold chicken stock and 1 tbsp fresh chopped tarragon, and stir until smoothly blended. Cover and chill for at least 30 minutes to allow the sauce to thicken and the flavours to infuse.

Shred the lettuce. Unless the peas are very young and tender, cook them and plunge them in cold water to cool quickly. Skin the chicken, carve it neatly, or bone and cut the flesh into bite-size pieces.

Arrange the lettuce in the centre of a serving dish and pile the cucumber and peas around the edges. Lay the chicken on the bed of lettuce, spoon some of the sauce over it and decorate with whole sprigs of tarragon. Serve the remaining tarragon cream in a sauce boat.

SERVES 6

TOFFEE CUSTARD

Caramel-flavoured puddings are always popular, and this simple farmhouse version of crème caramel is no exception.

1 pint/2½ cups (550 ml) milk
5 oz/scant ¾ cup (150 g) granulated sugar
4 large eggs
¼ pint/⅔ cup (150 ml) whipped cream or thickened
    yoghurt, or a mixture of the two
a few toasted almonds to garnish

Scald the milk and set it aside.

Melt the sugar in a large pan with 1 tbsp water, then cook until caramelised to a rich shade of gold. Away from the heat stir in a little of the milk—the mixture will bubble up furiously. Stir in the rest of the milk, and if necessary return the pan to the heat to dissolve the caramel completely.

Reserve one of the egg whites. Beat the rest of the eggs with a fork, and continue beating while pouring the caramel-flavoured milk on to them. Strain the mixture into a baking dish, cover the dish with foil and stand it in a roasting pan containing enough freshly boiled water to come halfway up the sides of the dish. Bake at 325°F (160°C), mark 3 for 40–50 minutes until set.

When the custard is cooked and cooled, whisk the reserved egg white and fold it into the cream and/or yoghurt mixture. Spoon the mixture over the custard and decorate with almonds.

SERVES 4–6

LEFT TO RIGHT: CUCUMBER CHICKEN WITH TARRAGON CREAM SAUCE, SPRING CLEAN SOUP (PAGE 16), FRESH HERB CHEESE (PAGE 16)

Good Eggs

One of the most delicious and versatile foods, in its own beautiful package is the egg. Eggs are an important ingredient in thousands of recipes. Often they are an "invisible" ingredient, working quietly and effectively to raise a cake or to thicken a sauce. Eggs are the major ingredient in many of our best loved dishes, the sort of soothing dish Nöel Coward had in mind when he said that all he wanted was "a little eggy something on a tray".

By "fresh" eggs I mean as fresh as you can buy them from a neighbouring farmer or friend, in other words a day or two old. I say this because, ironic though it may seem to anyone whose experience of eggs is limited to elderly supermarket offerings, an egg still warm from laying is *too* fresh for some cooking purposes. If fried, it will run and spit in the pan; if poached, the yolk may separate from the white; and if hard-boiled, the membrane clings to the egg so tightly that it is impossible to peel neatly.

As far as good eating is concerned, freshness matters a great deal more than whether an egg is free-range or battery, but if you want to be sure of buying genuine free-range eggs, look for the words "Free-range". Eggs sold as "Farm fresh eggs", "Barnyard eggs", "Nest box eggs" and so on, countrified though these terms may sound, do not mean free-range.

Nutritionally there is little difference between free-range and battery eggs, but the taste of free-range will vary a little. It is not true that brown eggs are better than white: the difference is simply in the breed of hen. Nor does the colour of the yolk reveal anything about the food value or the freshness of the egg.

The yolks of eggs are high in cholesterol and nutritionists recommend that we do not eat more than the equivalent of four yolks of hens' eggs per person per week. Remember that this is the maximum advised and that it includes "hidden" yolk as used in mayonnaise, custards, cakes, sauces and so on, as well as eggs eaten just as eggs.

Although hens' eggs are the most popular and the most widely available, the eggs of other domesticated birds also make very good eating and are well worth looking out for. At farm and cottage gates, and in delicatessens, you occasionally find the eggs of quail, pullet, bantam, guinea fowl, duck and goose.

Each of these eggs looks and tastes different, but generally speaking they can all be used to replace hens' eggs and can be used interchangeably in the following recipes. Substitute by weight rather than by number, bearing in mind that the average size 3 hen's egg weighs about 2 oz or 55 g.

There are some recipes for which each kind of egg seems particularly suitable or unsuitable. Size, richness, decorative qualities and cooking methods all need to be taken into account: having to crack open a dozen or so quails' eggs in order to make a single portion of scrambled eggs seems rather extravagant when just one or two hens' eggs will do. It makes better sense to reserve quails' eggs for occasions when you can show off the charm of their smallness or the decorative effect of their shells.

The following brief notes on eggs other than the familiar hen's egg may help you to consider the options.

Quails' eggs: about the size of a damson, these are the smallest eggs of which regular supplies are available, and the newest in that quails have only recently begun to be farmed. Shells are cream and brown speckled, lined with pale blue. Flavour is delicate, like a creamy hen's egg. Because they are so tiny, boiling is the most satisfactory cooking method, and because they are so pretty it is usual to let people shell the eggs for themselves. Quails' eggs are for elegant appetisers, not for square meals. Allow 4–6 eggs per person; boiling takes $1\frac{1}{2}$–2 minutes.

Guinea fowl eggs: these small eggs are about the same size as pullet and bantam eggs. They weigh about $1\frac{1}{4}$ oz (30 g). The shell is a matt, muddy pink—strangely plain looking when you consider the attractiveness of the guinea fowl—and very hard. Flavour is very delicate.

Pullet eggs: pullet is the name given to a young hen from the time she begins to lay till first moult. Pullet eggs rarely weigh more than $1\frac{1}{4}$ oz (30 g) but despite their scaled-down size, they have the full flavour of a hen's egg. Excellent for all cooking purposes, and particularly suitable for serving to young children or to elderly or ill people with small appetites.

Bantam eggs look and taste very much like pullets' eggs and are of similar weight. Again, good all-purpose eggs. Bantams are a miniature breed of hen.

Duck eggs weigh about 3 oz (75 g). The shell may be chalky-white or very pale blue. The yolk is golden-orange, the white is gelatinous and blue-tinged. Flavour is distinctive and very rich. Warnings against eating duck eggs unless hard-boiled are out of date: they stem from times when people were tempted to pick up stray eggs of indeterminate age found in the wild, which might have picked up germs through their porous shells. Duck owners today usually house their birds overnight; the eggs are normally laid during the hours of darkness and they are collected from the nesting boxes each morning. So, it is quite safe to use duck eggs for all cooking purposes—but the whites do not whip successfully to make meringues.

Goose eggs: very large with a thick, white shell, these weigh 6 oz (175 g) or sometimes quite a bit more. Fairly rich, but milder in flavour than duck eggs, goose eggs can be used for all cooking purposes. Because of their size they seem particularly appropriate for making omelettes and for scrambling. For soft-boiled eggs allow about 7 minutes cooking time.

Here are a few fun ideas and serving suggestions for special occasions:

EGGS-IN-A-NEST
Hard-boiled eggs take on special appeal if they are served in their shells and piled up in a nest made from moss raked from the lawn and decorated with a few daisies. Tiny decorative quails' eggs look spectacular, but pullet, bantam and guinea fowl eggs are also all suitable. Serve with brown bread-and-butter, and hand round celery salt and sweet paprika (for dipping quails' eggs) or a bowl of mayonnaise.

PARADISE EGGS
For a luxurious variation on *Eggs-in-a-nest*, shell the hard-boiled eggs and serve them in a nest of thinly sliced smoked salmon.

Watercress sauce goes well with this: process or finely chop 1 bunch of watercress into tiny green flecks, and mix with 2 tbsp each of mayonnaise and creamy yoghurt, and ½ tsp wholegrain mustard. Thin with 1 tbsp or more of milk.

MILLIONAIRE'S EGGS
Scramble goose or hens' eggs, saving the shells. Pile the cold scrambled eggs back into the shells and top with caviare—mock or real, depending on how much of a millionaire you really are. Serve with rye bread-and-butter and wedges of lemon or lime.

DECADENT EGGS
For the perfect brunch, serve soft-boiled eggs with asparagus instead of bread and butter "soldiers".

_M ANOR _H OUSE _E GGS

A rich tasting and ritzy little dish if the sauce is made with really good stock. An admirable dish for a luncheon party, in which case it will serve 3, or an elegant dinner party first course for 6 people.

butter, flour
4 fl oz/½ cup (125 ml) fish or shellfish stock
¼ pint/⅔ cup (150 ml) double (heavy) or whipping cream
Dijon mustard and fresh Parmesan cheese
lemon juice
6 guinea fowl eggs
2–2½ lb (900 g–1.1 kg) spinach, including a handful of sorrel if available
¼ lb (125 g) peeled prawns (shrimp)

Make a roux with ¼ oz/1½ tsp (7 g) butter and 1 tbsp flour. Blend in the stock and all but 1 tbsp of the cream. Bring to simmering point, stirring all the while.

Away from the heat, stir in 1 slightly rounded tsp mustard and 2 tbsp freshly grated Parmesan. Season to taste with salt and pepper and add a squeeze of lemon juice.

Put the sauce into the top part of a double boiler, drizzle the remaining cream over the sauce—do not stir it in—and cover with a lid. (The sauce can be made, and the spinach washed, well ahead of serving.)

Put 6 ramekins, or 1 large gratin dish, into the oven to warm. Soft- or hard-boil the eggs, shell them and keep them warm in a bowl of warm water.

Cook the spinach (and sorrel if using) until tender. Drain and squeeze out as much moisture as possible. Chop finely, season the spinach well and enrich it by stirring in a few tiny knobs of butter. Put the spinach into the warmed dish(es) and bury the eggs in it. Leave the eggs whole if soft-boiled; halve or quarter them if hard-boiled.

Put the top part of the double boiler over a pan of barely simmering water, and reheat the sauce gently but thoroughly, stirring all the while. Add most of the prawns, lightly chopped, and warm gently. Pour the sauce over the spinach and eggs. Garnish with the reserved whole prawns and then serve accompanied by fingers of hot toast or fried bread.

LEFT TO RIGHT: MILLIONAIRE'S EGGS (PAGE 21), MANOR HOUSE EGGS (PAGE 21)

HADDIE WITH EGGS AND OLIVES

A simple but exceedingly pleasing supper dish with a lovely combination of flavours and colours. Hot crusty bread and baked tomatoes (which can be cooked in the oven at the same time as the fish) make good accompaniments.

4 large fillets of smoked haddock
butter
12½ fl oz/1½ cups (350 ml) milk
½ bay leaf
2 duck eggs
a handful of parsley
1 oz/about 8 (25 g) small black (ripe) olives
plain (all-purpose) flour

Choose a baking dish which will just hold the fish fillets in a single layer. Butter it and lay the fish in it. Grind on some pepper and dot with 1 oz/¼ stick (25 g) butter. Pour on the cold milk and add half a bay leaf. Cover lightly and loosely with butter paper. Bake the fish for 20–25 minutes in an oven heated to 350°F (180°C), mark 4.

While the fish is cooking hard-boil and chop the eggs. Chop at least 5 tbsp parsley. Stone the olives. Put 1 oz/¼ stick (25 g) softened butter and 1½ tbsp flour in a saucer and mash together with a fork.

When baking time is up, strain the fishy-flavoured milk off the fish. Cover the fish again with the butter paper and keep it hot in the switched off oven. Bring the milk to simmering point in a small saucepan. Gradually stir in small pieces of the butter and flour mixture and continue simmering, stirring all the time, until the sauce is hot, thickened and perfectly smooth. Remove from heat and stir in most of the eggs and parsley. Check seasoning and pour the sauce over the fish. Garnish with the rest of the chopped eggs and parsley, scatter with the olives and serve.

SERVES 4

LITTLE CHEDDAR CUSTARDS

This is an attractive little first course and no trouble to make. Eggs are simply combined with cheese, milk and cream to make delectable little savoury custards—reminiscent of quiche but without the pastry. Little Cheddar Custards are small but rich tasting and high in cholesterol so they are best served just occasionally followed by a light, clean-tasting main course, preferably one that is vegetable based.

¼ lb (125 g) Farmhouse Cheddar cheese
3 large hens' eggs
freshly grated nutmeg
½ pint/1¼ cups (300 ml) milk
¼ pint/⅔ cup (150 ml) double (heavy) or whipping cream

Heat the oven to 325°F (170°C), mark 3, and bring a kettle to the boil.

Finely grate the cheese and lightly grease 6 small cocotte dishes or other such dishes suitable for baking eggs in. Beat the eggs with a fork in a large mixing bowl. Beat the cheese into the eggs and add a good seasoning of pepper and a grating of nutmeg. If the cheese is richly flavoured a seasoning of salt may well prove unnecessary, then beat in the cold milk and cream.

Ladle the mixture into the cocotte dishes, making sure each one gets its share of the cheese. Cover each little dish with a lid made from foil and stand them in a roasting pan. Pour into the roasting pan enough freshly boiled water to come half-way up the sides of the dishes. Slide the roasting pan very carefully into the oven and bake for 35–40 minutes until the custards are set to a soft creamy consistency.

Little Cheddar Custards are best served about 5 minutes after they come out of the oven, warm but not piping hot. I like to shake a little cayenne and paprika over them and to accompany them with oatcakes which have been gently warmed in the oven.

Little Cheddar Custards can also be served cold, in which case it is a nice idea to garnish them with a dollop of soured cream and perhaps a sprig of watercress.

SERVES 6

BABY SCOTCH EGGS

Scotch eggs made at home with a decent coating of good-quality meat, nicely seasoned and dusted with genuine breadcrumbs, will be a delicious revelation to anyone who has only eaten commercial varieties. Tiny eggs, as here, look pretty and it makes sense if you are catering for children or elderly people who might find a large egg, however delicious, just too much. Although Scotch eggs are excellent cold (and useful for packed lunches), they are perhaps best served as soon as cooked. I recommend them, hot and crisp from frying, on a bed of salad with baked potatoes on the side.

2 dozen quails' eggs
1½ lb (700 g) lean belly of pork (salt pork), boneless and de-rinded weight
¼ lb (125 g) onion
3 oz (75 g) Farmhouse Cheddar cheese
thyme, allspice and ground coriander seed
a little mustard and plain (all-purpose) flour
2 hens' eggs, beaten
¼ lb/1 cup (125 g) fine, toasted breadcrumbs
oil for deep-frying

Hard-boil the quails' eggs. Cool and shell them. Cube the pork and chop it very finely indeed in a food processor, or pass it twice through the fine blade of a mincer. Chop the onion as finely as possible and grate the cheese.

Thoroughly mix these two ingredients with the pork, together with about 2 tsp salt, plenty of pepper, at least 1 tsp dried thyme and a good pinch each of allspice and ground coriander. Process or pass the mixture through a mincer to make it quite smooth.

Divide the mixture into 24 pieces. Lay them on a damp work surface and flatten each into a circle large enough to wrap round a quail's egg. Spread each circle with a little mustard, place a shelled egg on top, then mould the sausage-meat firmly and evenly round the egg, making sure there are no cracks. Beat the hens' eggs. Roll the meat-wrapped quails' eggs in seasoned flour, dip in the beaten egg, and coat with breadcrumbs. Chill for at least 15 minutes to firm the coating.

Heat a pan of oil to 350°–360°F (180°–185°C) and deep-fry the eggs in batches until golden brown all over, turning them in the pan with a perforated spoon. They will take about 4 minutes to cook. Drain the eggs well and (if serving straight away) keep them hot in the oven while you cook the remainder.

MAKES 24

GENTLEMAN'S OMELETTE

Plump, greedily sauced omelettes were a feature of Victorian club menus. Served with grilled tomatoes and fresh hot toast, a dish like this makes a quick and substantial meal for one ravenous gentleman (or lady) or a light dish for 2 people.

1 goose egg
2 oz/1 cup (50 g) button or small cap mushrooms
2 lambs' kidneys
a little butter
2 tbsp good gravy
a dash of port, Madeira or dry sherry

Two pans are needed for cooking this dish: an ordinary frying pan for cooking the filling and for making the sauce, and a small omelette pan.

Break the egg into a bowl, season it lightly and beat briefly with a fork. Slice the mushrooms. Skin, core and slice the kidneys.

Heat the frying pan. Melt a piece of butter the size of a hazelnut. Add the mushrooms and sauté them, stirring and turning them to drive off moisture. Remove the mushrooms and keep them hot. Add a little more butter to the pan and fry the kidneys briefly—if cooked for long they will turn disagreeably leathery. Remove the kidneys and keep them hot. Put the frying pan to one side but first add the gravy and alcohol to it so there will be no delays when it comes to making the sauce.

Heat a little butter in the omelette pan and use the egg to make an omelette in the usual way. When nicely set underneath and still a little creamy on top, tip the kidneys and mushrooms on to one half of the omelette. Fold the other half of the omelette over the filling and gently slide the omelette on to a hot plate.

Quickly put the frying pan back on to the heat and stir vigorously to mix the gravy and the alcohol with the buttery meat juices sticking to the pan base. As soon as the sauce bubbles up, pour it over the omelette and serve straight away.

JADE STIR-FRY WITH RIBBON OMELETTES

Not authentic Chinese of course but very popular in my part of Wiltshire.

12 oz (350 g) courgettes (zucchini)
4 oz (125 g) each broccoli, mangetout (snow peas) and French beans
1 goose egg
peanut oil
fresh ginger and garlic (optional)
12 oz/3 cups (350 g) beansprouts
sesame oil
4–8 spring onions (scallions), split and curled in iced water
soy sauce and rice wine or sherry

First prepare the vegetables: coarsely grate the courgettes without peeling them. Break the broccoli into tiny sprigs. Top and tail the mangetout and French beans.

Beat the egg in a bowl with a little salt. Warm a small omelette pan and barely film the base with peanut oil. Add just enough egg to cover the base of the pan and cook it until set—it is more like making a pancake than cooking a traditional omelette. Flip the cooked omelette on to a plate and cook the rest of the egg in the same way. Then roll up each omelette tightly, like a cigarette, and snip into thin ribbons with scissors. Keep the omelettes warm in a low oven.

Put a spoonful or so of peanut oil into a wok. If you wish, add a little very finely chopped ginger and garlic, to scent the oil with their flavours. When the oil is very hot, tip in the prepared mangetout and French beans and stir and turn them over high heat for 1 minute before adding the beansprouts. Continue stirring and turning for a good minute more, before adding the broccoli. Cook for ½ minute, maximum, then add the courgettes. Go on turning and stir-frying the ingredients for a further ½ minute or so. Draw the pan away from the heat, sprinkle quickly with salt and a shake of sesame oil. Toss once more and serve straight away garnished with the spring onions and ribbon omelettes.

Offer separately plain boiled rice and a little bowl of sauce for sprinkling over the food. To make the sauce simply stir a dash of rice wine or sherry into a little soy sauce.

SERVES 4

COUNTRY GARDEN SALAD

This pretty salad with its delicious egg and herb sauce looks better served on a shallow dish than in a deep salad bowl. Alter proportions and substitute ingredients depending on what green vegetables are currently freshest and best. I sometimes include a few lightly steamed mangetout (snow peas), or French or runner beans, and I sometimes replace the chicken with prawns.

4 small chicken breast portions
fresh chopped parsley, chives, chervil, tarragon, mint and dill
olive oil and wine vinegar
3 thick slices of bread
1–1½ lb (450–700 g) asparagus
4–6 oz/about 1 cup (100–175 g) young peas
4 or 5 pullet or bantam eggs
¼ pint/⅔ cup (150 ml) thick cream or creamy yoghurt
1 cos (romaine) or butterhead lettuce
a small handful of tender young spinach or sorrel leaves
¼–½ cucumber

Poach the chicken breasts until just tender. Cool, skin and bone them. Cut the flesh into strips, put the strips into a bowl, and season with a little salt and pepper. Add 1 tbsp of each of the 6 fresh chopped herbs, a spoonful or two of olive oil and a few drops of wine vinegar. Toss gently, cover and set aside in a cool place.

Dice the bread, fry it in olive oil until golden, drain well and allow to become cold. Steam-boil the asparagus and dry it carefully in a clean napkin. The peas should be sufficiently young and tender to eat raw.

Hard-boil the eggs. Cool them and separate the yolks from the whites. Chop the whites and put aside. Pound the yolks to a paste with some salt, pepper and 3–4 tbsp cream or yoghurt. Carefully and slowly beat into the yolks 3 tbsp olive oil, then 1½ tbsp vinegar, then the rest of the cream and/or yoghurt. Check seasoning and add extra cream and/or yoghurt, oil or vinegar to taste.

Lay the lettuce and spinach or sorrel leaves in a shallow dish. Arrange the asparagus, chicken, sliced cucumber, chopped egg whites and peas on top, scattering the peas prettily here and there, and then garnish with croûtons made from the fried bread. Serve the sauce separately in a small bowl so that everyone can help themselves.

SERVES 6

BACK TO FRONT: JADE STIR-FRY WITH RIBBON OMELETTES, COUNTRY GARDEN SALAD

ST DAVID'S SUPPER

When the housekeeping budget is somewhat depleted for one reason or another, I turn to this cosy, economical and satisfying supper dish with a sigh of relief. For minimum wastage and tender eating, choose leeks with long, thin, white stems. Stout white parts are nearly always tough and the coarse greenery of leeks is never a pleasure to eat.

3 oz/¾ stick (75 g) butter
1½ lb (700 g) leeks, prepared weight
1–1½ duck eggs per person
½ lb (225 g) Farmhouse Cheddar cheese (or better still 50/50 Cheddar and Gruyère)
3 slices wholemeal (whole wheat) bread
2 tbsp plain (all-purpose) flour
1 pint/2½ cups (575 ml) milk

Melt the butter in a large saucepan. Add the leeks, which have been thinly sliced, carefully washed and dried. Turn them until each piece is lightly coated with butter. Cover the pan and leave to cook very gently for about 15 minutes. In the meantime, hard-boil the eggs. Put a large gratin or baking dish into the oven and switch the oven on to 375°F (190°C), mark 5. Scald the milk, grate the cheese and reduce the bread to crumbs.

When the leeks are tender, draw the pan away from the heat. Sprinkle on the flour and stir it in thoroughly. Add the hot milk, mix in well and return the pan to the heat. Bring to simmering point, stirring gently all the time. Half-cover the pan and leave to cook very slowly while you shell the eggs. Either leave them whole, or halve or quarter them if you prefer, and arrange in the hot baking dish.

Stir half the cheese into the leek sauce and season to taste. Pour the sauce over the eggs, cover the dish with foil and bake for 15 minutes until all the ingredients are piping hot. (If more convenient the dish can be prepared well ahead, in which case it will take nearer 25 minutes to heat through.)

Sprinkle the remaining grated cheese over the hot gratin and top with the breadcrumbs. Cook under a hot grill (broiler) for a few minutes so that the cheese melts and the crumbs become well toasted. Serve with plenty of good wholemeal bread to mop up the sauce, and with a large crisp green salad to temper the richness of the dish.

SERVES 4–6

PANPERDY WITH BACON

Panperdy is a corruption of "pain perdu", meaning lost or hidden bread. It is a very old recipe and the eggs were originally highly seasoned with spices such as cloves, nutmeg and cinnamon. This is my modern-day savoury version, which makes a delicious light supper dish. Children love the surprise of discovering the fried bread hidden under its eggy disguise. I also make a sweet version—replacing the bacon and herbs with slices of dessert apple, peeled, fried lightly in butter until hot, and dusted with cinnamon sugar.

4 hens' eggs
2 small, fairly thick slices of bread
¼ lb (125 g) streaky bacon
a little butter
1 tbsp chopped fresh parsley
1 tbsp chopped fresh chives

Crack the eggs into a mixing bowl. Season them lightly and beat briefly with a fork. Cut the crusts off the bread. De-rind the bacon and cut it into snippets.

Fry the bacon gently until the fat begins to run. Increase the heat a little and crisp the bacon. Remove it with a slotted spoon and keep hot.

Add a good knob of butter to the pan and, when the butter foam dies down, add the bread. Fry it until golden and crisp on one side. Turn the bread over and fry it for a few seconds only, to colour it lightly, before pouring on half the beaten eggs. Allow the egg to spread around the bread and leave to cook fairly gently for 2 minutes or so until the underside of the bread is golden and the bottom of the egg is completely set.

Scatter the bacon over the bread and pour on the rest of the beaten egg to hide the bread completely. Transfer the pan to a hot grill (broiler) and cook just long enough for the egg mixture to puff up and set softly. Sprinkle on the herbs and serve straight from the pan.

SERVES 2

COOK'S NOTEBOOK

There was a time not too long ago when it was thought smart to ignore what went on in the kitchen. In grand houses kitchen quarters were carefully concealed behind a green baize door, just as children were relegated to the nursery upstairs. In smaller and less affluent households, kitchen and dining room were physically closer but still kept as separate as possible.

The idea of trying to divorce things culinary from the rest of living seems crazy. Cooking and eating are intertwined and together they form a basic and essential part of our lives. We all recognise this now and the kitchen is no longer shunned as a necessary annexe to the house but welcomed as central to it. The cottage kitchen has always been like this of course: a warm and friendly place filled with exuberant aromas that shout their glory to the rafters and draw everyone into the kitchen like moths to a flame, with hunger pangs deliciously keened.

There is something irresistible about dishes that act as their own dinner gong. I mean things like Sunday's roast chicken or a succulent garlic-studded leg of lamb.

Piggy in the Orchard is just such a dish, making mouths water as it bubbles enticingly in the pan. Cube 1½ lb (700 g) lean pork and season it well with pepper and some crushed garlic, but no salt. Leave for several hours (preferably a day) to absorb flavours. Fry 2 large thinly sliced onions for a few minutes in dripping or butter in a big sauté pan. Add the pork and brown it well. Pour on scant 1 pint/2½ cups (550 ml) dry cider and let the mixture simmer gently for 20 minutes without a lid, just stirring occasionally. Add 3 Cox's apples, peeled, cored and cut into chunks, plus a very generous lump of butter and some sage, thyme or rosemary. Cook for another 20 minutes or until pork and onions are cooked and the liquid has reduced to a few syrupy spoonfuls. Season with salt and serve with creamy mashed potatoes and a crisp watercress salad.

In the bosom of the family, in a noisy, cheerful kitchen living room, cooking is kept in proper perspective, seen simply as a natural expression of our deep-rooted feelings about domesticity. Fancy emulations of cheffery and slapdash non-cookery seem equally out of place. Here in the family kitchen the gentle art of simple home cooking lives on. Cooking methods are deliberately straightforward—sufficiently simple to cook while keeping half an eye on a small child. Ingredients are similarly modest —with strong emphasis on local produce in season.

Vegetables play an important part in this sort of cooking, and *Country Cabbage* is delicious proof that not all country people are guilty of the old English sin of killing vegetables by drowning. Soften a small, very finely chopped onion in 1 tbsp oil in a large non-stick frying pan. Add another tbsp oil and 2 leeks sliced so finely that they fall into ribbony shreds. Stir to film with fat. Add 1¼ lb (600 g) finely shredded savoy cabbage and stir and turn the ingredients again. Season, cover tightly and cook very gently, stirring occasionally, until the vegetables are cooked —neither too crisp nor too soft.

Like vegetables, fish is best served straight from the pan the moment it is cooked, and I wouldn't dream of starting to fry *Fisherman's Trout* until the fisherman had changed out of his waders and was ready to sit down at the table. What makes this dish so good is the trick of drying the trout skin and rubbing it gently with plenty of pepper and a little flour before cooking. Fry the fish in foaming clarified butter for 4–5 minutes on each side, lightly pressing the fish down into the pan so the skin crisps to a deliciously piquant golden brown. Remove the fish to hot plates. Quickly fry some bacon snippets or flaked almonds or both. Add salt, pepper, and lemon, tip the contents of the pan over the fish, and serve.

Here is a fun recipe with which to celebrate Easter: *Lemon Soufflé Omelette*. Unlike a soufflé proper, it is very quick and easy to cook. In keeping with the traditions of good home cooking, it is made from ordinary, inexpensive ingredients. It is simply delicious and gloriously spring-like, filling the kitchen with the joyously sharp scent of fresh lemons. Separate 6 eggs. Beat the yolks with 2 rounded tbsp sugar and the juice and zest of a lemon. Whisk the whites until stiff, fold in the flavoured yolks and slide the mixture into a large buttery frying pan. Cook over gentle heat until the omelette begins to bubble and rise in the pan. Then transfer the pan to a hot grill (broiler) and continue cooking until the omelette is beautifully puffed up, just set and lightly browned. Serve at once, straight from the pan.

Baking Bread

There is something really satisfying about cutting into a loaf of bread which you yourself have baked. The pleasure stems partly from our perception of bread as the most basic and timeless of foods—and partly from sheer greed: freshly baked bread with its warm yeasty smell is utterly irresistible.

The idea of bread making may be compelling but few cooks actually bake bread frequently. I cannot help feeling that more would do so if they felt it was a practical proposition, not some lengthy, mysterious and arcane process demanding the patient mastery of time-consuming skills.

In practice, thanks to modern aids like food mixers, processors and new easy-blend yeast, bread making has become an enormously simplified process. No great labour, no obscure art best suited to those with time on their hands, but a straightforward and hugely rewarding kitchen craft which really can be made to fit in with the routine of today's busy lifestyles.

Bread making is something at which even the novice cook can achieve shining success very quickly, for unlike other areas of baking, it is an essentially down-to-earth business. Whereas successful pastry making and cake decoration depend on acquiring a certain lightness and delicacy of touch, bread making does not. In fact bread dough positively relishes a bit of rough handling.

The whole beauty of home-made bread lies in its home-madeness. Its individuality singles it out from the shop-bought product and you know exactly what has gone into its making. Taste is what counts. No need to strive to shape your wholemeal cob into a perfect round; no need to worry if it rises slightly less than the average baker's offering. As long as it tastes good these things do not matter. In fact a certain lack of factory-line uniformity only adds to the charm and appetite appeal of home-made bread and serves to underline the fact that it is a natural and wholesome product.

FLOURS

Wholemeal flour is just that—whole meal or 100 per cent of the edible grain. It is the most healthy flour. Because it contains all the bran (fibre) of the wheat, it does not rise dramatically but produces loaves of fairly close crumb and slightly chewy texture; because it contains all the wheatgerm it is rich and nutty in flavour. As such wholemeal flour makes delicious plain bread—but it has almost too much character to be used with great success as the sole flour in flavoured breads.

Strong white bread flour has less to recommend it from a health point of view (it contains only 72–76 per cent of the grain, with practically all the bran and wheatgerm removed) but it is valuable in bread making nonetheless. Its lack of bran makes for light loaves, tender crumbed and rising to billowy heights; its lack of wheatgerm gives it delicate flavour. The inclusion of some white flour in flavoured breads can be very desirable, helping to provide a gentle background note which allows added ingredients, such as spices, to step into the limelight and be shown off to best advantage. Look for the word "unbleached" on the label if you want to avoid chemically whitened flour.

Brown flour is to all intents and purposes a halfway-house flour. Being partially refined (it contains 80–90 per cent of the grain) its nutritional value and its character lie somewhere between those of wholemeal flour and those of white flour.

Granary flour is a hybrid flour, containing some malted grain and crushed wheat, blended by the miller according to his own recipe. Its maltiness and the fact that it contains little nuggets to bite into are making it increasingly popular.

Stone-ground flour is any flour so labelled has been ground the traditional way, between stones instead of modern steel rollers, which means it retains more nutrients. Stone-ground flour is, so to speak, the farinaceous equivalent of virgin oil, pure and expensive.

EASY-BLEND YEAST

One of the big breakthroughs in bread making in recent years has been the introduction of easy-blend yeast. This product really lives up to its name. Unlike conventional dried yeast it does not need to be reconstituted in liquid first: you simply mix it directly with the flour.

KNEADING HELP

Even more appealing to many cooks is the news that it is not obligatory to devote 15 minutes or so to mixing and kneading the dough by hand. Thorough kneading *is* essential but it does not have to be done by you; a machine will do it. Some people wax lyrical about the pleasures of kneading by hand. Therapeutic it may be—just occasionally—but more often it seems a frankly boring and long

HERB GARDEN BREAD (PAGE 33)

drawn-out chore. If you're going to make bread frequently you will probably welcome the chance to hand over this time-consuming task to a machine which is capable of doing the job as efficiently, or even better than you could, and will do it much more quickly.

Either an electric food mixer with a dough hook, or a robust food processor is suitable. It is important to follow your manufacturer's instructions closely and to keep always within the dough capacity of your machine, remembering that the maximum recommended quantity of flour to be used usually refers to white flour. Allow one-third less for wholemeal—its bran content makes it harder to knead and so puts more strain on the machine.

SINGLE V DOUBLE RISE

Yeast bread doughs are traditionally risen twice before baking, and this is one point on which I am a stickler for tradition—because I firmly believe that the twice-risen method produces bread that is infinitely superior in texture and taste.

It is true that modern recipes for so-called beginner's bread, one-rise quick time bread and the like, can shorten the time lapse between starting to make a loaf and sitting down to eat it. But single rise breads really are no easier to make and most of the extra time involved in making double rise bread is *rising* time—during which, of course, the cook does not need to be on duty. On occasions when speed is of the essence, I suggest you forget about baking with yeast and make soda bread instead.

Soda bread is a quick and simple recipe: mix $\frac{3}{4}$ lb/2$\frac{1}{3}$ cups (350 g) wholemeal flour and $\frac{1}{4}$ lb/scant 1 cup (100 g) soft white flour—not bread making flour—with 1 tsp each salt and bicarbonate of soda (baking soda). Rub in 2 oz/$\frac{1}{2}$ stick (50 g) butter and bind to a soft dough with $\frac{1}{4}$ pint/$\frac{2}{3}$ cup (150 ml) each milk and yoghurt. Shape the dough into a large flat bun, score it with a deep cross and bake on a floured sheet at 425°F (220°C), mark 7 for 30–35 minutes.

All the following recipes are for twice-risen breads. The basic method is described at length in the master recipe for Daily Bread. The other recipes go into detail only when there is an important variation of method.

DAILY BREAD

Nutritionists say we should eat more bread and in particular they urge us to eat more wholemeal bread because of its high fibre content. I agree, not only on grounds of good health but also of good taste. It is not for nothing that this recipe is called Daily Bread: it is a plain wholemeal loaf to bake and to eat on a day-in-day-out basis.

1$\frac{1}{2}$ lb/scant 5 cups (700 g) wholemeal (whole wheat) flour
1 × $\frac{1}{4}$ oz (7 g) sachet easy-blend yeast
2 tsp salt
$\frac{3}{4}$ pint/scant 2 cups (400 ml) warm water
1 tbsp vegetable oil or $\frac{1}{2}$ oz/1 tbsp (15 g) butter

Mixing and kneading: mix the dry ingredients in the bowl of a food mixer or processor. Put the water into a jug (1 part boiling to 2 parts cold is about the right temperature) and add the oil or butter. If using butter, dice it and put it into the jug before adding the cold water so it melts quickly. Add the contents of the jug to the dry ingredients and mix and knead to a smooth, elastic dough—follow the manufacturer's instruction leaflet closely for details.

First rise: after kneading, the dough should be covered and set aside to rise until doubled in size. I cover the dough by putting it into a lightly oiled polythene bag, a large one to allow plenty of room for the dough to expand, and secure the bag at the neck. How long the dough will take to rise can vary considerably and the following timings should be treated as approximations only. Go by the size of the dough, not by the clock, and be patient. If the dough looks disappointingly small when the time is up, leave it a while longer.

In a warm place: 74°F (23°C) (eg airing cupboard or sunny windowsill)	**approx 1 hour**
At average room temperature: 65–70°F (18–20°C)	**1$\frac{1}{2}$–2 hours**
Traditional north-facing larder or other cold room	**8–12 hours**
In a refrigerator	**up to 24 hours**

(If dough rises in a fridge it must return to room temperature before knocking back.)

Aim for a slow or quick rise, depending on what fits in best with your timetable. Many cooks find an 8–12 hour, cool, overnight rise most convenient and it is generally agreed that this produces the best bread. Others find a quick rise suits them far better.

Knocking back and re-kneading: when the dough is well risen it will be puffy and soft. It needs to be knocked back to get rid of air pockets, and another brief kneading to make it smooth and elastic again. These processes can be done electrically but they are very quick and easy to do by hand.

To knock back the dough, give it two or three hefty punches with your fist (now that *is* therapeutic) and flatten it with your knuckles to reduce it to its original size, then knead it for just a minute or two. The most popular way to knead involves repeating the following actions over and over again: starting at the far side of the dough, use your fingers to pull and fold the mass of dough towards you, slap it down on to the work surface, then push it away with the heels of your hands. There is no need to follow this routine slavishly. Knead the dough (pummel, push and stretch it) however you fancy and be as rough as you like.

Shaping: The dough is now ready for shaping.

For a traditional tin loaf: the easiest way to get a good shape is to flatten the dough to an oblong about 3 times the width of the tin. Fold the dough in 3 and turn it seam side down. Tuck the ends under, drop the dough into the tin and push it down lightly around the sides to give the loaf a nicely rounded top. The tin should be greased and the dough should half to two-thirds fill it. For this recipe you need 1 large 2 lb (900 g) or 2 small 1 lb (450 g) loaf tins.

For a round loaf: shape the dough into a rough ball. Then smooth the top by drawing the dough down with your fingers and folding it underneath, repeatedly. Place the ball of dough on a greased baking sheet and flatten it slightly into a cob shape, or drop it into a greased cake tin of suitable size.

Proving (2nd rising): slide the baking sheet or bread tin into the lightly greased polythene bag and set aside to rise again. How long this second rising will take depends on room temperature, on the volume and richness of the dough. In a warm kitchen a plain loaf made with 1½ lb/scant 5 cups (700 g) wholemeal flour will probably take about 1 hour, a smaller loaf 50 minutes.

Baking: bake plain wholemeal loaves in an oven preheated to 425°F (220°C), mark 7. A large loaf will need about 45 minutes to cook through and a small loaf about 35 minutes but again, it is impossible to give hard and fast timings. Use your eyes, nose and ears as well as the clock to guide you. A loaf is ready when it begins to shrink away from the sides of the tin. When out of the tin, it should sound hollow, like a drum, if tapped on the base. Loaves which have been baked in a tin are best returned to the oven for a few minutes after unmoulding to colour the sides and underside.

Last but by no means least, always cool freshly baked bread on a wire rack: this allows steam to escape and lets you enjoy the aroma—surely the best of all kitchen smells.

HERB GARDEN BREAD

Although best made with fresh herbs (the smell wafting from the oven is mouthwatering), this recipe works well using dried herbs. In this case, I suggest ½ tsp each dried oregano, thyme and powdered rosemary plus a crushed garlic clove. Fragrant and shaped like a miniature French loaf, Herb Garden Bread is just right for sandwiches that are in effect a complete lunchbox. Split the bread lengthways as for a sandwich, but leaving one side uncut to act as a hinge, and scoop out a little of the crumb to make a boat-shaped hollow. Thread long skewers with well-marinated kebab ingredients. Baste and grill (broil) in the usual way. As soon as cooked, strip the kebab ingredients off the skewers and into the bread hollows. Season well, add a little watercress or shredded lettuce if there is room, and quickly fold the bread "lid" over the filling to encase it completely. Wrap each sandwich separately in plenty of foil and weigh down lightly for at least 2 hours.

1 lb/generous 3 cups (450 g) brown flour
1 × ¼ oz (7 g) sachet easy-blend yeast
1 tsp salt
½ pint/1¼ cups (275 ml) warm water
1½ tbsp olive or sunflower oil
1 large garlic clove or 3–4 spring onions (scallions)
2 tbsp fresh chopped parsley
1 tbsp each fresh chopped mint, thyme and
    marjoram
1 tsp fresh chopped tarragon

Using a food mixer or processor mix and knead the flour, yeast, salt, water and oil to a smooth dough. Cover and leave to rise until doubled in size: this will take about 1 hour in a warm place.

Knock back the risen dough and knead it briefly. Crush the garlic, or finely chop the spring onions (green parts as well as white), and mix with the herbs, then work the flavourings into the dough.

Cut the dough into 3 or more pieces and roll each into a long thin sausage shape, like a small French stick. Lay the shaped dough on a greased baking sheet, cover and set aside to prove until well risen—about 1 hour in a warm place.

Brush the top of the dough with a little water and sprinkle with wheat flakes or kibbled wheat as garnish or leave it plain. Bake at 425°F (220°C), mark 7 for 20–25 minutes or until cooked through.

SAFFRON BREAD (PAGE 36)

SAFFRON BREAD

With its shiny crust and tender yellow crumb, this is a very handsome bread which tastes as brilliant as it looks. The saffron flavouring means it is especially well suited to serving with fish dishes but it also goes well with white meats and I like to use saffron breadcrumbs to replace some of the usual flour when making dumplings to serve with chicken and rabbit stews. Freshly made Saffron Bread, still slightly warm from the oven, is splendid with Mediterranean-style fish soups and stews, and equally good with traditional British treats, such as dressed crab and tiny brown Morecambe Bay shrimps. Toast Saffron Bread for serving with fish pâtés. Cube it and fry it and use it instead of mashed potato to top a special fish pie. Make it into breadcrumbs and use it for coating fish cakes and other fish for frying. Saffron Bread makes deliciously colourful sandwiches. Try it with flakes of poached cod and shreds of lettuce nicely moistened with dill mayonnaise and garnished with a slice of lemon or lime and a few prawns. Try it too for a sweet treat thickly spread with cream cheese and generously sprinkled with sultanas, raisins and chopped candied peel.

2 packets saffron
7 fl oz/scant 1 cup (200 ml) milk and water mixed
12 oz/scant 2½ cups (350 g) strong white bread flour
4 oz/scant 1 cup (100 g) brown flour
1 × ¼ oz (7 g) sachet easy-blend yeast
1½ tsp salt
2 eggs, beaten (reserve a little to glaze)

If the saffron is in the form of stamens rather than powder, first pound it to a fine powder with a pestle and mortar. Put the powdered saffron into a small pan with the milk and water (the liquids should be cold) and bring very slowly to boiling point. Set the pan to one side until the saffron liquid has cooled to blood temperature.

Using a food mixer or processor mix and knead the flavoured liquid with the other ingredients to a soft dough. Cover and leave to rise until doubled in size: this will take about 1 hour in a warm place.

Knock back the risen dough and knead it lightly. Shape the dough and put it in a greased tin—a large (2 lb/900 g) loaf tin or a 7 in (18 cm) round cake tin. Cover and leave to prove until well risen: this will take 1 hour or so in a warm place. Glaze with the reserved beaten egg and bake at 375°F (190°C), mark 5 for about 35 minutes. Remove the loaf from the tin and bake for a few minutes more.

POTATO BREAD

The use of potato in bread making has a lot to recommend it. The potato is invisible and you cannot taste it but it helps the action of the yeast and results in a particularly light, moist bread. Potato Bread makes excellent toast and is ideal for pocket sandwiches. These are tailor-made for packed lunches. To make a pocket sandwich, first toast a very thick slice of bread. Cut the crust off one edge only, and slip the knife blade horizontally into the centre of the crumb exposed by the removal of the crust. Cut gently to create a large pocket, taking care not to pierce the toasted surface of the bread. Spread a little Marmite inside the pocket. Drop in 2 or 3 bacon rashers which have been grilled until crisp, then cut into snippets. Add a little of the hot melted bacon fat, some watercress or a little salad cress or a shredded lettuce leaf or two. The sandwich should be fairly generously filled but not bursting at the seams.

For a delicious meatless filling, replace bacon and bacon fat with sautéed mushrooms anointed with best olive oil and seasoned with ground coriander seeds and a little garlic.

1 medium-sized potato (a floury variety)
½ lb/generous 1½ cups (225 g) wholemeal (whole wheat) flour
½ lb/generous 1½ cups (225 g) brown flour
1 × ¼ oz (7 g) sachet easy-blend yeast
1½ tsp salt
8 fl oz/1 cup (225 ml) warm potato cooking water
1 oz/¼ stick (25 g) butter

Scrub the potato but do not peel it. Steam or boil it, taking care not to overcook. Drain the potato well and save some of the cooking water to use as the liquid for mixing the bread dough. Peel away and discard the potato skin. Sieve the flesh smoothly: 6–7 oz/¾–scant 1 cup (175–200 g) cooked weight is needed for this recipe.

Using a food mixer or processor mix and knead all the ingredients to a smooth and elastic dough. Cover the dough and set it aside to rise until doubled in size: this will take about 40 minutes in a warm place.

Knock back the risen dough and knead it again briefly. Shape the dough and put it into 1 large (2 lb/900 g) or 2 small (1 lb/450 g) greased loaf tins. Cover and leave to prove until well risen: this will take 30 minutes or so in a warm place.

Bake the bread at 450°F (230°C), mark 8 for 10 minutes. Reduce oven temperature to 400°F (200°C), mark 6 and continue baking until the loaves are fully cooked—about 20 minutes for small loaves or 30 minutes for a large loaf.

COOK'S NOTEBOOK

Some city folk seem to be under the impression that the average country cook is virtually slave to a freezer, doomed to spend half her waking hours feeding its rapacious appetite with pheasants, trout and, above all else, with the marrows, Brussels sprouts and other vegetables of which, like some carelessly breeding rabbit, she has produced too many.

I suppose there are people who shoot and fish with a view to filling their freezers, and there may be some who deliberately grow more fruit and vegetables than they could possibly need for immediate eating, but I am certainly not among their number. Having said that, I must add that I do own a freezer and find it very useful. As a lover of such things as coffee and cheese, and living some miles from good sources of supply, the prime value of the freezer for me is as an extended shopping basket for delicatessen-type foods. Coffee freezes beautifully, the whole beans miraculously retaining their fresh roast aroma for months. There's no need to thaw them before grinding and brewing.

Curd cheese and other low-fat soft fresh cheeses have too much moisture and too little fat content to freeze successfully, but all other types of cheese freeze pretty well. The process is particularly useful for creamy blue cheeses like Bresse Bleu and Dolcelatte and for soft matured cheeses like Brie and Camembert, all of which are so good to eat when they are just right and so unappetising when they are immature or over the top. The trick about freezing cheese is to freeze it when it reaches the perfect stage for eating and no

sooner, because cheese cannot continue to ripen after defrosting. Once defrosted, cheese is best eaten up quickly.

Brie and Camembert are naturals for *French Rarebits*, which are quite different in character from toasted cheese dishes made with Cheddar, Lancashire or Leicester but just as delicious. Lightly toast thick soft slices of bread on one side only, spread the untoasted side with a smear of good chutney, cover with thin slices of rindless ripe cheese and grill (broil) gently until just melted and gooey. Sprinkle with sunflower seeds and flash briefly under the grill again until the seeds are toasted and the cheese lightly gilded. Serve with a large, crisp salad.

A freezer can be the cook's best friend when it comes to coping with leftovers.

My personal Achilles' heel about leftovers used to be chicken. I divide whole chickens into joints and often prefer to skin the meat before cooking, particularly if it is to be served in a delicate sauce. Making stock with the carcass and gizzards has long been second nature to me—so easy, so rewarding, and have you looked recently at the ingredients list on a packet of commercial stock cubes? My problem was what to do with the chicken skin. For years I did nothing except chuck it into the dustbin. Now I wrap it, freeze it, and look forward to the day when I will have saved enough to make *Frizzy Chicken Salad*. To make this you need the skin of six breasts of chicken, or an equivalent amount taken from other joints or whole chickens. First prepare a large salad, using

ingredients which will provide an agreeably clean-tasting foil for the fatty rich chicken. I suggest a handful or two of thinnings taken from rows of lettuces, leeks and other greenery in the vegetable garden, a few very young dandelion leaves (but don't use dandelion after the first day of June: it will be disagreeably bitter and coarse) and a smattering of sorrel for sharpness, some spinach perhaps, and a little rocket or watercress for extra pep. Dress the salad with a squeeze of lemon and a dash of olive oil. Then cut the defrosted chicken skin into snippets and deep fry it quickly until beautifully crisp and golden. Drain it, sprinkle it with salt, toss it with the salad, and serve with plenty of good bread on the side.

Other "naturals" for freezing are what I call half-ready dishes. By this I mean dishes which have to be, or can sensibly be, set aside at some point during the preparation and cooking process, for example a fruit crumble. When making a crumble with rhubarb I sometimes include slivers of stem ginger. With tart green gooseberries I might use elderflower. You could bury a vanilla pod among sunny freckled apricots, but I prefer to make a special topping: *Apricot Crunch* is made just like any other crumble but uses oatmeal and nuts instead of flour. To cover 1 lb (459 g) apricots I allow 4 oz/ 1⅓ cups (100 g) coarse oatmeal and 2 oz/⅔ cup (50 g) each medium oatmeal, butter and demerara sugar, plus 3 oz/¾ cup (75 g) flaked almonds. Sprinkle the topping mixture over the fruit and freeze uncooked.

CHEESY GRANARY BREAD

Cut this rich cheesy round loaf across, into regular slices, or cut it into wedges like a cake, depending on how you want to use it. Slices make a fine basis for hot pizza-type snacks. Wedges are good to munch with salads for sit-down lunches at home—a sunny tomato and black olive salad partners the bread particularly well.

For a practical and portable version of this lunch dish, cut the loaf in half horizontally to make two large rounds. Rub both cut surfaces with garlic and brush generously with olive oil. Pile on to the bottom half lots of thinly sliced tomatoes and some onion. Season with salt and pepper and scatter with chopped and stoned olives, gherkins, capers and/or fresh herbs. The mixture should be very piquant. Sandwich the two rounds of bread together again and place under a weighted plate for at least 1 hour so the filling is pressed into the bread and the crumb blots up the juices. Wrap the loaf well, pack it at the bottom of the picnic basket, and cut into wedges with a sharp knife just before serving.

ABOVE: DAILY BREAD (PAGE 32)
RIGHT: CHEESY GRANARY BREAD

10 oz/2 cups (275 g) granary flour
6 oz/generous 1 cup (175 g) brown flour
$1 \times \frac{1}{4}$ oz (7 g) sachet easy-blend yeast
1 tsp salt
1 tsp pale muscovado sugar
$\frac{1}{2}$ pint/$1\frac{1}{4}$ cups (275 ml) warm water
$\frac{1}{2}$ oz/1 tbsp (15 g) butter
7 oz/$1\frac{3}{4}$ cups (200 g) grated Farmhouse Cheddar cheese

Using a food mixer or processor mix and knead everything except the cheese to a smooth dough. Cover and leave to rise until doubled in size: this will take about 1 hour in a warm place.

Knock back the risen dough and knead it briefly, gradually working in 4 oz/1 cup (125 g) of the cheese. Roll out the dough to an oblong about 8 × 18 inches (20 × 45 cm) and lay it on the work surface with one of the short ends facing you. Sprinkle nearly half the remaining cheese on to the centre of the dough and fold the bottom third of dough over it. Sprinkle most of the rest of the cheese on top and fold the final third of dough over it. Then pat and tuck the dough, curving and shaping it gently to fit a lightly greased 8 inch (20 cm) round cake tin. Cover and prove until well risen—about $1\frac{1}{4}$ hours in a warm place.

Sprinkle the last of the cheese over the top of the dough, and bake the bread at 400°F (200°C), mark 6 for 35 minutes or so in the tin and for a further few minutes out of the tin.

NUTTY HARVEST BREAD

This is the most popular bread I bake, the sort of bread to which one can easily become addicted. It is dense of crumb, nutty and chewy, thick with protein-rich goodies, and it goes well with both sweet and savoury foods. Because it is such nutritious bread I often serve it just as it is, with no butter or anything else to spread on it. Served this way, it makes a fine and well-balanced accompaniment to fresh vegetable soups, delicate stir-fries, simple oven-baked pulse dishes, crisp salads and so on.

Small children like Nutty Harvest Bread spread with fresh low-fat soft cheese that has had grated carrots and a few chopped dates or raisins mixed into it. For more sophisticated palates try serving a good hunk of the bread with a rollmop, grated apple and watercress salad; or with a small joint of smoked chicken accompanied by a ripe juicy pear, fresh figs or muscatel grapes.

15 oz/3 cups (425 g) wholemeal (whole wheat)
    flour
1 oz/generous ⅓ cup (25 g) medium oatmeal
1 × ¼ oz (7 g) sachet easy-blend yeast
1 tsp salt
1 tsp pale muscovado sugar
1 tbsp sunflower oil
½ pint/1¼ cups (275 ml) warm water
1 oz/2 tbsp (25 g) each of any three of the following:
    sunflower seeds, pumpkin seeds, sesame seeds, walnut
    kernels, hazelnut kernels

Using a food mixer or processor mix and knead the flour, oatmeal, yeast, salt, sugar, oil and warm water to a smooth and elastic dough.

Cover the dough with oiled polythene and leave it to rise until doubled in size: this will take about 1 hour in a warm place.

While the dough is rising, chop fairly coarsely the hazelnuts and/or walnuts if planning to use them, and lightly toast the nuts and seeds of your choice to intensify their flavours.

Knock back the risen dough and knead it briefly, gradually working in your chosen nuts and seeds. Shape the dough into a baton-shaped loaf and place it on a greased baking sheet, or put it into a large (2 lb/900 g) greased loaf tin. Cover and leave to prove until well risen: this will take about 40 minutes in a warm place. Bake at 425°F (220°C), mark 7 for 35 minutes or so until the loaf is cooked through.

SPICY CINNAMON BREAD

This bread is for lovers of cinnamon. The recipe was inspired by thoughts of country house teas in days gone by when muffins were regularly toasted in front of the fire, buttered and sprinkled with cinnamon sugar. It is a bread which toasts well (I love it spread with marmalade for breakfast), and it makes unusually good sandwiches when spread with roughly mashed banana instead of butter. Children love these sandwiches particularly if you add a little honey or slices of kiwi fruit or a few halved and seeded grapes as well as some lightly toasted almonds.

Spicy Cinnamon Bread is also excellent for giving a new lease of life to a whole host of old-fashioned puddings. Its spiciness adds distinction to dishes like apple charlotte, Eve's pudding and autumnal versions of summer pudding made with blackberries, damsons or plums. Best of all perhaps is the idea of using Spicy Cinnamon Bread for a slightly different bread and butter pudding—spread with a little rum butter and sprinkled lavishly with dried fruits it is sensational.

10 oz/2 cups (300 g) strong white bread flour
6 oz/generous 1 cup (150 g) wholemeal (whole wheat) or
    brown flour
1 × ¼ oz (7 g) sachet easy-blend yeast
1 tsp salt
1 tsp pale muscovado sugar
2 tsp ground cinnamon
1 slightly heaped tsp ground allspice
½ pint/1¼ cups (275 ml) mixed warm milk and water
2 oz/½ stick (50 g) butter
beaten egg to glaze

Using a food mixer or processor mix and knead to a soft dough all the ingredients except the beaten egg. Cover the dough and leave it to rise until doubled in size: this will take about 50 minutes in a warm place.

Knock back the risen dough and knead it briefly. Put it into a large (2 lb/900 g) loaf tin or shape into a plait (braid).

To make a plait, cut the dough into three equal pieces and roll each into a sausage shape about 16 inches (40 cm) long. Pinch the three strands together at one end, plait loosely and pinch together at the other end. Lay the dough on a greased baking sheet.

Cover and leave to prove until well risen: this will take about 45 minutes in a warm place.

Glaze the top of the loaf with a little beaten egg and bake at 425°F (220°C), mark 7 for about 35 minutes or until cooked through.

BROWN RICE BREAD

Cooks have long been using rice in bread making, the original purpose being to keep costs down when bread flour was expensive. Brown Rice Bread has excellent keeping qualities, it is agreeably moist and its flavour is gentle and unobtrusive. For these reasons, albeit a good all-purpose bread, it is particularly useful for serving with foods that are delicate tasting and prone to dry out easily. For example, the crumbs are ideal for making stuffings for poultry and fish. It is an admirable bread for sandwiches and makes an attractive sandwich cake for special picnics and buffet lunches. To make a sandwich cake, first remove the crusts from the top and bottom of the loaf, then slice the loaf lengthways into 5 slices. Spread 4 of the slices with butter, or better still with mayonnaise, and cover with colourful and tasty fillings: I suggest one layer of chicken and toasted almonds; one of ham and tongue; and two of avocado mashed with plenty of chives and other chopped fresh herbs. Put the loaf back together again, wrap it well and chill it thoroughly for at least 1 hour before slicing.

3 oz/½ cup (85 g) brown rice
12 oz/scant 2½ cups (350 g) wholemeal (whole wheat) flour
6 oz/generous 1 cup (150 g) strong white bread flour
1 × ¼ oz (7 g) sachet easy-blend yeast
1 tsp salt
9 fl oz/generous 1 cup (230 ml) warm water
1 tbsp sunflower oil

Cook the rice in double its volume of salted water. Then mix the warm, freshly cooked rice with the flours.

Using a food mixer or processor add the remaining ingredients and mix and knead to a soft dough. Cover the dough and leave it to rise until doubled in size: this will take about 1 hour in a warm place.

Knock back the risen dough and knead it very briefly indeed, adding a little more flour if it is too soft to handle easily. Shape it and put it into a large (2 lb/900 g) greased loaf tin. Cover and prove until well risen: about 1 hour in a warm place. Bake at 425°F (220°C), mark 7 for about 40 minutes in the tin, and for a further 10–15 minutes out of the tin, or until cooked through.

SUMMER

Summer is a time for celebration with
the fresh taste of young vegetables,
green herbs and scarlet fruits. We plan
picnics or laze in the garden with
friends; bees buzz and ice clinks
in tall glasses.

Young Vegetables

When the new season's vegetables begin to burgeon in the garden my heart lifts with anticipation. As soon as they are ready to eat, the pleasure increases: I am filled with gardener's pride and not a little greed. Never mind that each pea has cost the earth to grow; nothing can equal the delicate green flavours and textures of vegetables that are truly young and fresh.

It is only by growing your own that you can feast on mangetout peas (snow peas) that really are mangetout, not *mangemoitié* as most commercial offerings ought to be called. Squeaky fresh sorrel and slim stringless French beans are the prerogative of gardeners. So too are truly sappy sweet spinach, asparagus and radishes: a trio of vegetables which seem to lose half their juicy fresh charm within an hour of picking.

More often than not you cannot buy potatoes the size of marbles, or carrots and courgettes (zucchini) as small as children's fingers, or broad (fava) beans so babyish that they can be eaten as they are in the downy pods that cradle them.

Early season vegetables like these are glorious treats and they deserve pride of place on everyone's menus. They are natural stars of the kitchen, crying out to be shown off as dishes in their own right. It seems a shame to restrict them to the shy understudy role of mere accompaniments to meat.

As I see it, the cook's task is to choose and to cook these special vegetables with extra tender loving care—and to know when to leave well alone. Too much adornment can overpower their delicate flavours and textures. Brief, simple cooking is best: it allows the youth and beauty of the vegetables to speak for themselves.

To treat vegetables in this way, serving them as appetisers and using them as the basis for main-course dishes, makes good sense in all sorts of ways. It makes life deliciously easy for the cook. It ties in well with our natural taste for lighter foods when the weather begins to warm up. Last, but by no means least, it is in keeping with today's trend towards less meat in the diet—whether for reasons of health, cost or concern about animals.

The recipes and ideas which follow are vegetable not vegetarian in concept. I have deliberately avoided the earnest and frankly stodgy effects associated with much vegetarian fare. Such things seem to me far too heavy-handed to complement the essentially delicate qualities of early season vegetables.

Equally inappropriate, in my view, is the ultra-lightweight approach favoured by exponents of *cuisine miniscule*. I mean the pretentious and over-priced style of cookery in which, say, two or three very lightly cooked beans and a single coriander leaf are artfully displayed on an octagonal plate. This may or may not look chic but it certainly spells starvation rations to anyone with a halfway decent appetite.

The quantities suggested here are not stingy, and the cooking methods might be described as whole-some and traditional—although I have tried to resist the traditional country temptation to use lashings of butter or cream with everything. I see all these recipes as being useful for vegetable-loving cooks who are keen to make best use of top-quality fresh produce in season. Some of the recipes may have special appeal for cooks who wish to en-courage their families towards healthier eating.

The way to wean convinced carnivores into eating less meat and more fibre-rich vegetables is by delicious temptation, not by dictatorial insistence. Men and children tend to be very conservative about food. Tell them you are serving a meatless meal, or even drop a hint that you plan to cook in a more health-conscious manner, and the chances are they will start complaining they are being deprived of "proper" meals.

On the other hand, if you don't breathe a word about what you are up to, but just quietly and gradually incorporate more vegetable-based dishes into your menus, the chances are that the family will tuck in happily and come back for second helpings without being aware of the altered emphasis.

None of the recipes given here are suitable for serving to vegans, and the two which include fish are unsuitable for strict vegetarians, but I have found that semi-vegetarian friends have welcomed all of these dishes. (By semi-vegetarian I mean those who never eat red meat, but who eat fish freely and a little poultry occasionally.)

Vegetarians, whether strict or semi, are rapidly growing in number, yet their tastes rarely seem to be taken into account. All too often the vegetarian is made to feel the odd one out. Simply by passing their plates when carving the meat, and plying them instead with larger helpings of vegetable accompani-ments, is frankly rather inhospitable; while cooking a separate menu especially for guests can embarrass just as much. Preparing one meal that everyone can share in, whether vegetarian or not, is more friendly to all concerned and really is no hardship for those who love meat.

None of this is to imply that carnivores ought to consider becoming vegetarians. My aim is simply to aid awareness of just how delicious vegetable cookery can be. There is no better time than now to put these ideas to the test, for vegetables are at their most exquisite at this time of year.

Buttered Radishes, or *radis au beurre* as it is more often called, is so simple that it can hardly be called a recipe. The radishes must be tender, crisp and plump, and they must be brought to table within minutes of picking and rinsing under the tap. Serve them with wafer-thin curls of sweet butter, sea salt to flake over them, and planty of good bread to munch on the side. This is wonderfully satisfying food, needing only the addition of good soup to make a fine lunch for a summer's day.

Sucky Peas is another country treat of childhood memory. For this you need peas so young that they barely swell the pod. Boil them, without topping, tailing or shelling them, so the peas are steamed inside the pods. Drain well and serve with a bowl of melted butter. The idea is to pick up the peas by the stalk end, to dip them into the butter, then nibble and suck out the peas and the succulent flesh of the pod.

Asparagus Tatties is a dish to remember for times when just a few asparagus spears are ready to harvest and several people have gathered to share them. The trick is to cook baby new potatoes in the same pan as the asparagus (so the potatoes absorb and are flavoured by the asparagus liquid). Serve the two vegetables on the same plate with a little melted butter, and a scattering of fried breadcrumbs for crunchy contrast.

Broad Beans in Pyjamas can only be made with broad beans harvested long before what commercial growers would consider to be profitable maturity. Do not pod the beans, just top, tail and cut them into short lengths. Boil them until they're just tender, coat with thin creamy béchamel sauce and season with lemon juice and fresh chopped tarragon.

Sucky Peas and *Broad Beans in Pyjamas* are best boiled but I usually prefer to steam vegetables. Steaming is a slightly longer process but gentler and better for retaining textures and vitamins. Irrespective of whether vegetables are steamed or boiled, always save the cooking water for stocks or soups. To throw it away is tantamount to chucking both money and vitamins down the drain.

SUMMER MEDLEY

This is a wonderfully versatile recipe and the best way I know to use thin asparagus or tender stalks trimmed from fat asparagus tips. Broccoli stalks can be used instead if preferred, and frozen petits pois when fresh young peas are no longer available. The optional inclusion of a little pasta helps to stretch the dish attractively and makes it more nutritious. Using the full quantity of pasta turns it from a vegetable dish into a pasta dish, but doesn't rob the dish of its fresh quality or make it heavy.

1 large cucumber
6–7 oz/about 1½ cups (175–200 g) shelled weight young
    peas
about 6 oz (175 g) cooked asparagus or broccoli stalks
lemon juice, sugar, fresh mint, 2 oz/½ stick (50 g) butter
up to ¼ pint/⅔ cup (150 ml) water saved from cooking the
    asparagus or broccoli
1 tsp cornflour (cornstarch)
2–4 oz/½–1 cup (60–120 g) macaroni (optional)

Peel and seed the cucumber and cut the flesh into sticks about 1 inch (2.5 cm) long and ¼–½ inch (1–1.2 cm) wide. If using fresh peas shell them. If using frozen peas defrost them by pouring boiling water over them. Cut the pre-cooked asparagus or the broccoli stalks into small pieces.

Put the butter into a flameproof casserole or heavy-based saucepan. Add a good grinding of black pepper, a little salt, about ½ tsp each sugar and freshly squeezed lemon juice and a sprig of mint.

Pour on some cooking water saved from cooking the asparagus or broccoli: ¼ pint/⅔ cup (150 ml) will be needed if using fresh peas, only about 4 tsp for frozen peas. Bring to the boil. Add the peas (if fresh) and the cucumber and bring quickly back to the boil.

Cover tightly and simmer gently, just shaking the pan occasionally, for 4–5 minutes or until the vegetables are nearly tender. Then add the cooked and diced asparagus or broccoli stalks—and the frozen peas if using them. Cover again and continue cooking very gently for a couple of minutes or so, just shaking the pan occasionally, until the vegetables are all hot and tender.

Stir in the cornflour, mixed to a paste with cold water, and cook for 1 minute, stirring, until the buttery vegetable juices are thickened to a smooth light sauce. Check and adjust seasoning to taste. Add freshly boiled and drained pasta if you wish.
SERVES 3–6

CREAMY COURGETTES

Made with cream, this is an exquisitely delicate dish. Made using equal quantities of cream and yoghurt, it is still very good—and less wickedly rich. I do not recommend the use of yoghurt only: it seems to spoil the essentially gentle character of the dish. Courgettes and cucumber are often salted before cooking to extract some of their copious water content. Using salt mixed with sugar and tarragon vinegar, as here, is just as effective and leaves the vegetables with more delicate flavour. If you want to serve this dish as a first course, I suggest cooking it in individual dishes—large ramekins or cocottes or tiny soufflé dishes.

1 lb 2 oz (500 g) courgettes (zucchini)
caster (superfine) sugar and tarragon vinegar
1 large egg
½ pint/1¼ cups (300 ml) whipping cream, or half
　quantity each cream and creamy yoghurt (Greek
　strained yoghurt is ideal; home-made must be
　stabilised or it will curdle in cooking)
a little Parmesan cheese (optional)

Top and tail the courgettes but do not peel them. Grate them coarsely into a bowl. Add ½ tsp salt, 1 tsp caster sugar and 1 tsp tarragon vinegar. Toss lightly and leave for half an hour or more to draw off some of the moisture from the courgettes.

Drain well in a sieve, then squeeze the courgettes very firmly with your hands, a small batch at a time, to extract as much juice as possible—it is amazing just how much liquid they will yield up. Put the by now rather compressed courgette gratings into a shallow lightly buttered gratin dish and "fluff" them with a fork.

Lightly beat together the egg and the cream—and the yoghurt if including it. Season well with pepper and a pinch of salt. Add a small spoonful of freshly grated Parmesan cheese if you wish—I suggest omitting the cheese if yoghurt is used. A few tarragon or basil leaves make lovely additions in season.

Gently but thoroughly stir the creamy mixture into the courgettes and bake at 400°F (200°C), mark 6 for 20–25 minutes until the mixture is just set but still a little creamy in the centre.
SERVES 4–6

Cooking with yoghurt: home-made yoghurt and most commercial brands tend to curdle or separate out when subjected to prolonged or high heat in cooking. (Some Greek-strained yoghurt seems to be the exception to this rule.) To minimise the risk of yoghurt curdling in cooking, it can be stabilised as follows: put a little cornflour (1 tsp per ½ pint/1¼ cups/275 ml yoghurt) into a saucepan and gradually blend in the yoghurt. Place over low heat and stir continuously, in one direction only, until boiling point is reached. Stabilised yoghurt will keep for several days if covered and refrigerated as soon as it is cooled.

SUFFOLK PRAWNS WITH LETTUCE

This delightful and delicately flavoured combination of ingredients makes a lovely light main course for 3–4 people, and it is one of those useful recipes which take only a few minutes to prepare and cook. Early in the season, before really large well-hearted lettuces are available, I have successfully used two or more small lettuces instead, or literally dozens of lettuce thinnings. The important thing is to use a crisp variety of lettuce. Soft, floppy-leaved cabbage or butterhead varieties are unsuitable.

1 garlic clove
1 inch (2.5 cm) fresh ginger root
¼ pint/⅔ cup (150 ml) double (heavy) cream or Greek
　strained yoghurt, or a mixture of the two
1 very large Webbs, cos (romaine) or iceberg lettuce
1 oz/¼ stick (25 g) clarified or unsalted butter
1 lb (450 g) cooked and peeled prawns (shrimp)

Crush the garlic. Peel and chop the ginger as finely as possible. Stir both flavourings into the cream or yoghurt, or a mixture of the two, and add a generous seasoning of salt and pepper. Set the mixture aside to infuse. Ideally, this should be done an hour or more ahead of cooking.

Shred the lettuce. Choose a very large heavy-based sauté pan or similar and thoroughly heat it. Add the butter cut up into small pieces. When the butter foam dies down, shake and tilt the pan to film the whole of the interior with fat. Add the lettuce and stir and turn it over high heat for a few seconds until every shred glistens with butter.

Then quickly tip into the pan first the flavoured cream or yoghurt mixture, then the prawns. Cook over medium heat, stirring and turning the ingredients frequently, for 2–3 minutes until prawns and lettuce are thoroughly hot and cream and vegetable juices have amalgamated to make a bubbling sauce. Serve without delay, straight from the pan on very hot plates, accompanied by good crusty bread that has been warmed in the oven. Lots of bread will be needed (or plain boiled rice if you prefer) to mop up the copious quantities of thin, creamy lettuce-juice sauce.

FRESH TOMATO CHARLOTTE

A very fresh-tasting dish. Although best made with sweet home-grown tomatoes, this is an excellent recipe for making the most of bland commercially grown tomatoes. Serve it as an attractive appetiser with lots of good bread to soak up the flavoursome juices. Or serve it as a vegetable accompaniment to grilled chicken or fish. For a vegetarian main course try it with a vegetable soufflé omelette, some rice or lentils, and a dish of yoghurt.

1½ lb (700 g) tomatoes
1 oz/¼ stick (25 g) butter
sugar, lemon juice and fresh mint
mayonnaise (shop bought will do)
Greek yoghurt
about 1½ oz/¾ cup (40 g) fresh wholemeal (whole wheat)
    breadcrumbs

Put the tomatoes into a bowl. Pour on boiling water to cover and leave for a few seconds to loosen the skins. Drain, peel and slice the tomatoes.

Butter a baking dish or four *oeuf sur le plat* dishes. Put half the tomatoes in the dish(es) arranging them just overlapping, like tiles. Sprinkle them with sea salt and a good grinding of black pepper. Add a little lemon juice and sugar (about ½ tsp of each) and a scattering of torn mint leaves. I recommend at least a dozen mint leaves. Cover with remaining tomato slices, again arranging them slightly overlapping, like tiles.

Dot with the rest of the butter and bake uncovered until warm and tender—about 25 minutes at 325°F (160°C), mark 3.

Towards the end of this time mix together 3 tbsp each of mayonnaise and Greek yoghurt. (If you prefer a sharper-flavoured dish, use a more acid variety of commercial yoghurt or make your own.)

Spoon the mixture thinly and evenly over the top of the tomato slices and slide the dish(es) back into the oven for 5 or so minutes more to heat through the topping. Finally, scatter the fresh breadcrumbs thinly and evenly over the top to hide completely the contents of the dish(es) and cook briefly under a hot grill (broiler) until the crumbs are well toasted and nicely browned.

SERVES 4

FRICASSY OF SPINACH

Lemon juice and cinnamon are used here to flavour lightly cooked spinach in a fresh and original way, and the mixture is finished with a little egg. The result is a surprisingly filling vegetable dish. Serve it hot, accompanied by Fresh Tomato Charlotte and plenty of good bread for an enticing meal without meat. Leftovers, should there be any, can be served cold, packed into pitta bread with sliced tomatoes for a lunchbox sandwich.

1½ lb (700 g) spinach
1 large onion
2 tbsp virgin olive oil
lemon juice and ground cinnamon
5 large eggs

Thoroughly wash the spinach in cold, salted water having first discarded any tough stems. Tear large leaves in half. Shake the spinach as dry as possible if you intend to steam it—a large steamer basket will be needed. If you prefer to cook the spinach in its own juices, simply drain it well and put it into a pan.

Beat the eggs in a bowl with a seasoning of salt and pepper. Chop the onion very finely and fry to soften it in the olive oil in a non-stick frying pan measuring 7–8 inches (18–20 cm) in diameter. Everything up to this stage can usefully be done well ahead.

Cook the spinach in its own juices or by steaming. Use high heat and turn the leaves fairly frequently to encourage even cooking. Do not cook for too long: draw the pan away from the heat as soon as the leaves are just wilted and tender. If the spinach has been steamed, stand the steamer basket on a draining board for a minute or two to let the steam evaporate. If the spinach was cooked in its own juices press the spinach in a sieve with a wooden spoon. Either way, save the liquid for delicious stocks and soups.

Add the spinach to the frying pan and stir to mix the spinach and onion well. Season with a tsp or so of lemon juice, plenty of pepper, some salt and two or more generous pinches of ground cinnamon.

Pour the beaten egg into the pan and cook over medium-low heat until the egg begins to set and a few surface bubbles begin to appear, then slide the pan under a fairly hot grill (broiler) and continue cooking until the top of the fricassy is softly set like an omelette.

SERVES 4–6

FENNEL AND ALMOND PILAFF

Fennel and almonds make admirable partners. The faint anise flavour and juicy texture of the vegetable provide a lovely foil for crunchy almonds, whose nutty sweetness is intensified here by frying until golden. This pilaff makes a very substantial main course for 4 or 5 people. If you want something lighter, suitable for serving as a first course or as a straightforward vegetable dish, omit the rice. Instead, tip the hot freshly cooked vegetables and almonds out of the frying pan and into a gratin dish. Scatter a few breadcrumbs over the top and a generous sprinkling of freshly grated Parmesan cheese, then slide the dish under a hot grill until the cheese has melted and the breadcrumbs are nicely toasted.

1¼ pints/generous 3 cups (700 ml) well flavoured stock
½ lb/1⅓ cups (225 g) long-grain brown rice
about 1¾ lb (800 g) Florentine fennel
olive oil and butter
3 oz/¾ cup (75 g) split almonds

Bring the stock to a fast boil and stir in the rice. Immediately reduce the heat as low as possible. Cover the pan with a well fitting lid and simmer until the rice is tender and has absorbed all or almost all of the liquid, which takes about 35 minutes.

Trim the fennel, reserving feathery fronds for garnish and scraping the bulbs to remove any fibrous threads. I find it easiest to pare away the threads with a potato peeler. Cut the flesh into generous bite-size chunks and fry them gently in a little butter and olive oil for 12 minutes or so until nearly tender. It is best to use a large frying pan so that the vegetables are not piled too deeply and so will cook fairly quickly.

Add the almonds to the frying pan and increase the heat slightly. Fry, stirring and turning the ingredients fairly frequently until both the fennel and almonds are streaked with gold. Season well with salt and pepper.

If there is any liquid left in the rice pan when the rice is cooked, drain it off. Add the cooked rice to the frying pan and immediately draw the frying pan away from the heat. Toss to mix the ingredients well and add a few small dice of butter to enrich the mixture. Garnish with the chopped fronds of the fennel and serve straight away.

EMERALD AND IVORY

This is a pretty dish: the vegetables are arranged like a Victorian posy of flowers and various accompaniments are handed round in separate bowls so that everyone can help themselves. It makes a substantial first course for 8 or can be served with plenty of good bread and a tomato salad on the side for a light lunch for 4–6. In the latter case I might use more eggs.

3 eggs
4 oz/2 cups (125 g) fresh wholemeal (whole wheat)
    breadcrumbs
butter
1 fine cauliflower
¾–1 lb (350–450 g) broccoli
lemon juice or anchovy essence (extract)
1 garlic clove (optional)

Hard-boil the eggs, shell and chop them quite finely. Fry the breadcrumbs, using just a little butter for toasty not greasy results, and keep hot in a low oven.

Trim the cauliflower neatly, keeping it whole and making a cross-shaped cut in the stalk. Sit the cauliflower in a steamer basket, place over boiling water, cover tightly and cook until tender. This should take a maximum of 20 minutes.

Cook the broccoli separately, starting it a little later as it needs no more than 10 minutes to become tender. Separate the florets from the stalks. Steam the florets and cook the stalks in the boiling water under the steamer basket. The stalks are not needed for this recipe but they can usefully be saved, together with the cooking liquor, for use in another recipe such as *Summer Medley*, page 45.

When the vegetables are nearly ready, melt about 4 oz/1 stick (125 g) butter. Season it with pepper and about 2 tsp lemon juice or a little anchovy essence. You can add a crushed garlic clove if you wish.

As soon as the vegetables are cooked, mop up any beads of moisture clinging to them with kitchen paper. Slide the cauliflower on to a warmed serving dish and arrange the broccoli prettily in a circle all round it. Quickly spoon a little hot melted butter over the cauliflower and scatter a little each of the chopped hard-boiled eggs and fried breadcrumbs.

Serve straight away, handing round the rest of the butter, breadcrumbs and eggs in three separate small bowls.

COOK'S NOTEBOOK

In summer an alarm clock is superfluous. I am woken at first light by the sibilant chirruping gossip of house martins nesting under the eaves, and I get up willingly. Dressing-gowned and sipping my first cup of tea, I go into the garden to relish this most exhilarating time of day, when God's in His heaven and all's right with the world. I fill the bird bath with fresh water and breathe in the cool fragrance of unfurling grass and flowers. Then I cast keen eyes over the vegetables neatly tucked up in their beds and, spurred on by a little greedy sampling, I plan the day's menus. It's a daily ritual and the pleasure never seems to diminish.

As every cook-gardener has the good fortune to know, the first produce of summer is exquisite, quite different from the vegetables of commerce which are rarely harvested until maximum maturity is reached.

Who can deny the simple pleasure of gleaning at noon a colanderful of squeaky fresh spinach for lunch; or sitting on the kitchen steps at dusk, leisurely chatting while shelling young peas for supper? It's only by growing them yourself that you can enjoy courgettes (zucchini) as small as fingers, with skin so tender that it peels away at the flick of a nail.

At the beginning of the season, a first glance at the kitchen garden may suggest that there is insufficient of any one vegetable to be worth picking. In truth it's not so. A scant handful of early spinach would of course melt to insignificance if cooked, but use the leaves raw, mix them with a few thinnings taken from a row of lettuce, add a couple of very young dandelion leaves and a scattering of fried bread croûtons, and you have a deliciously appetising little *garden salad*.

When vegetables are as young and tender as this, they deserve to be served very simply, as a dish in their own right. Asparagus and globe artichokes are invariably accorded such respect. Why not other, humbler vegetables? Carrots, runner beans, courgettes and leek thinnings all respond beautifully to such treatment. I steam them whole, just long enough to render them more digestible, and serve them warm with an hollandaise sauce for dipping.

Once the growing season gets into full swing, vegetables become central to meals, no longer peripheral. In some areas Whitsun is still celebrated with a traditional dish of *Pot Roast Duck with Minted Peas*. Put a bunch of mint inside a plump fresh duck weighing about 5 lb (2.3 kg). Prick the skin all over—but not the flesh—and fry the bird gently until it exudes a good quantity of fat. Pour off the fat and save it. Increase the heat and continue frying the duck until its skin is a crackle of gold, then place the bird breast-side down in a stewpot. Pour on about ½ pint/1¼ cups (300 ml) giblet stock, add a curl of lemon peel, cover tightly and simmer for a good hour. Turn the duck over, add a large shredded lettuce, about 1½ lb/scant 5 cups (700 g) shelled peas and a seasoning of salt and pepper. Re-cover and continue simmering until the duck is perfectly tender. This is wonderful just as it is, but even better if served, as Hannah Glasse recommended, with a sauce made by beating a little of the well reduced cooking liquor with 2 egg yolks, a few spoonfuls of thick cream and a generous handful of fresh chopped mint.

By late summer the cook's problem is quite simply how to keep pace with the growth rate in the garden. More and more people are turning to the freezer as a means of coping, but I cannot bring myself to do that. I find the production line tasks of batch blanching and packaging too soulless and too tedious. Besides, I like to stay in step with the seasons—I have no appetite for garden peas in December or sprouts in June.

I find salvation in the old solutions and get out my soup pan gratefully. The green flecked purée of *Courgette Soup*, spiked with a hint of basil and Parmesan, is a particular favourite of mine. Bolted lettuces, too bitter to eat raw, are transformed by shredding and simmering with herbs and a good home-made light stock for *Chiffonade Soup*.

Courgettes that think they are marrows are best treated as such: steamed and served with a fresh tomato sauce, or stuffed and baked. Any mixture generally used for stuffing tomatoes, peppers or aubergines (eggplant) is suitable. Most luscious of all is the concoction quaintly called *Velvet Slippers*. Blanch the courgettes and halve them lengthways. Scoop out some of the flesh, dry it well in a clean tea towel or absorbent paper, chop it and mix it with 1 part fresh breadcrumbs, 2 parts grated Cheddar and 4 parts cream cheese. Bind with egg yolks, season well, use to stuff the "slippers" and bake in a buttered dish in a moderate oven for about ½ hour.

Scarlet Fruits

When scarlet berries, currants and cherries first come into season, the pleasure of them is so intense that it seems silly to adorn them. When the soft-fruit season is in full swing, we may feel blasé about feasting on strawberries, raspberries and redcurrants plain and simple. Then is the time to start slicing, crushing and whipping the fruits into sweet summer puddings. But at first I want nothing better than to serve and to eat the fruits just as they are so that their glorious colours and shapes and their luscious sharp-sweet juiciness can be enjoyed to the full.

Midsummer Dip is my idea of the ideal dish with which to celebrate the scarlet fruit season. It consists simply of three bowls or baskets of whole raw fruit: one piled high with perfect strawberries, the second with a tumbling pyramid of sweet cherries, and the third filled with jewel-like bunches of fresh and frosted redcurrants. Alongside the fruit is soft cheese—a billowing bowl of snowy white *fromage blanc*—and, mindful of sweet-toothed friends, there is a little bowl of sugar. The idea is for everyone to help themselves, picking up pieces of fruit by the stalk to nibble just as they are, or to moisten in a glass of wine, or to dip into the creamy soft cheese before eating—each according to his or her taste.

A dish like this is so simple it scarcely warrants being called a recipe, but its simplicity is what makes it so stunning. There is something exhilarating about brilliantly fresh, top-quality fruit in generous quantity. And generous you certainly can afford to be, because there won't be any wastage: fruit that is served on the stalk retains its freshness well and any that is not eaten can be re-used the next day in other dishes. Fruit that has been hulled, or otherwise treated does not, of course, give the cook the same options.

Midsummer Dip would make a fine finale for a dinner party and it is just right for the sort of long, lazy summer lunch in the garden that I enjoy so much. I mean the sort of lunch party that has no rigid menu structure but is a bit like a picnic. This is my favourite way of entertaining in summer: casual, timeless occasions when friends gather together to relax in sun-dappled shade on green grass under the pale watercolour blue of an English sky. Leisurely chat and shared dipping and sipping as we linger late into the afternoon and the air is filled with the agreeable sounds of laughter, bumble bees and the clink of ice in tall glasses. Occasions like these call for nothing but the best, but nothing fancy. It seems appropriate that the emphasis should be on fresh garden produce: generous salads, light savoury mousses, crusty bread, farmhouse cheeses and lots of scarlet fruits.

For **Midsummer Dip** for 6–8 people I allow at least 2 lb (1 kilo) each of strawberries, raspberries and redcurrants. It is the contrast of crunchy crystalline casing and tart juicy fruit that makes frosted redcurrants irresistible. As well as using them for Midsummer Dip, I use them to garnish all sorts of summer ice-creams, puddings and cakes, and I sometimes serve them, like chocolate, to nibble with after-dinner coffee. How to make frosted redcurrants is described in Queen of Jellies, page 56. Store them in an airtight tin and they will keep for 2–3 days.

Why, you might ask, do I suggest serving fromage blanc with Midsummer Dip when thick, softly whipped cream is the traditional British accompaniment to scarlet fruits. It's a question of taste. Stick to cream if you wish. Having made an effort to cut down on animal fats in recent years, I now find thick cream on its own just too rich and cloying. It seems to suffocate the tastebuds and to act as a blanket, masking the sweetness and fragrance of the fruit, rather than heightening its beauty. Now I usually lighten the richness by mixing cream with whisked egg white or yoghurt. Sometimes it is preferable to use only yoghurt or fromage blanc, no cream. Sometimes it may be best to avoid dairy products of any sort. Fruit tastes fruitiest without any fat.

Fromage blanc, fromage frais or soft fresh cheese in plain English, is essentially the sort of simple cheese country cooks used to make—like rice pudding—whenever there was surplus milk in the house. Now there are two commercial brands whose fresh tastes and light textures make them perfect partners for scarlet fruits. The best comes from Neal's Yard Dairy in London.

Another delicious alternative to full cream is yoghurt. I don't mean low-fat yoghurt made with skimmed or semi-skimmed milk powder. I mean creamy yoghurt made at home with whole (unskimmed) milk, or the Greek strained yoghurt now on sale in many supermarkets. Greek yoghurts are available in two versions: strained and ewes' milk. With fat contents of 10 per cent and 6 per cent respectively, they are decidedly high-fat compared to other yoghurts but their balance of richness and sharpness is very appealing—even to professed yoghurt-haters. When you consider that double, whipping and single creams have fat contents of 48,

35 and 18 per cent respectively, you can see there is a considerable saving to be made by using Greek strained yoghurt in place of any of these.

A year ago I mostly used Greek strained yoghurt. Now I am beginning to find even that pretty rich and I rate the lower fat ewes' milk version as the more useful and pleasing of the two. If you are ahead of me in the healthy game of learning to appreciate less fatty foods, then you may well wish to use ewes' milk yoghurt (6 per cent fat) in recipes where I specify strained yoghurt (10 per cent fat), and to use low-fat yoghurt (up to 2 per cent fat) where I specify ewes' milk yoghurt. If, on the other hand, you and yours are only just beginning to say no to thick cream, then you may prefer, for a few months, to use a little more cream and a little less yoghurt or fromage blanc in each of the recipes that follow.

Just as a bland blanket of cream can distract from the fruitiness of fruit, so flavourings can overpower rather than enhance if indiscriminately used. A mere whisper of raspberry-flavoured framboise, orange curaçao, kirsch or white rum can add a subtle extra dimension to scarlet fruit dishes, but it is a mistake to think that if a spoonful of liqueur is good news then a glassful will be even better. Be sparing, too, with triple-distilled flower waters. They are a romantic notion and their effects can be exquisite, adding magical fragrance to scarlet fruit desserts. But they are potent. Slosh them on and they will make fruit taste boudoir stale instead of fresh from the garden.

A light splash of wine, grape juice or cider can be delicious with strawberries or raspberries. I like even better the Italian trick of dressing scarlet fruits with a *soupçon* of freshly squeezed orange and lemon and a pinch of sugar. Barely moisten the fruits, toss gently and set aside for half an hour. What is so clever about this treatment is the way it seems to sharpen the overblown flavour of any over-ripe berries you may be using and, para-doxically, to round out the thin taste of slightly under-ripe fruits. At the end of half an hour the fruits will taste perfectly of themselves and will gleam like rubies. They will have yielded up some of their scarlet juices and these will have mingled with the citrus and sugar to make the lightest and fruitiest of syrups imaginable—a truly exciting taste of summer.

RED QUIVER

Anyone who loves the taste of raspberries and redcurrants but dislikes the pips will find this recipe a delight. It is one of my favourite red fruit puddings. I love it because it looks handsome, tastes delicious and somehow gives the impression that you might have spent hours preparing it. The truth of the matter is that it is very quick and easy to make, involving hardly any cooking at all. What is more, it is not an unduly expensive dessert and it is healthily devoid of animal fats.

$\frac{3}{4}$ lb (350 g) redcurrants
$\frac{3}{4}$ lb (350 g) raspberries or loganberries
5 oz/scant $\frac{3}{4}$ cup (150 g) granulated sugar
1 pint/$2\frac{1}{2}$ cups (575 ml) hot water
3 tbsp cornflour (cornstarch)
creamy yoghurt or fromage blanc to garnish (optional)

Reserve a scant 100 g ($\frac{1}{4}$ lb) of each fruit for garnish. Put the rest into a food processor or blender. Dissolve the sugar in the hot water, stirring the liquid until it no longer feels gritty. Pour the sweetened liquid over the fruit and reduce to a purée, then rub the purée through a sieve to de-seed.

Measure the cornflour into a saucepan. Blend in a little of the fruit purée to make a paste, then stir in the rest of the purée. Cook over moderate heat, stirring continuously, until the mixture is smooth and reaches simmering point. Simmer for 1 minute then set aside for 10–15 minutes to cool slightly. Taste the mixture and add a little more sugar or a squeeze of lemon juice if you think it necessary.

Pour the ruby red mixture into small bowls or glasses, filling them to within $\frac{1}{2}$ inch (1 cm) of the tops, and leave in a cold larder for a few hours until set to a delicate jelly.

Top each pudding with a dollop of creamy yoghurt or *fromage blanc* (I like the contrast of colours and tastes) and garnish with the reserved berries and currants just before serving. Little almond biscuits go well with this dish.
SERVES 8

MIDSUMMER DIP (PAGE 50)

TRIFLING RASPBERRIES

This is an old-fashioned trifle, or whim-wham, with a deliciously high fruit content and no alcohol, although I doubt you will miss the latter. A thick layer of crushed berries is spread over the sponge base, and covered by a proper egg custard then topped with a spectacular rich raspberry syllabub, which may be garlanded with blue flowers. Cream is essential to this recipe but loganberries or blackberries could be used instead of raspberries.

½ lb (225 g) or more slightly stale Victoria sponge
3 large oranges
1¼ lb (600 g) raspberries
1 whole egg plus 1 extra yolk
1 oz/2 tbsp (scant 25 g) caster (superfine) and icing (confectioners') sugars
½ pint/1¼ cups (275 ml) single (light) cream
lemon juice and triple distilled rose water
½ pint/1¼ cups (275 ml) double (heavy) cream
a few fresh borage flowers or crystallised violets to garnish (optional)

Break the sponge cake into pieces and arrange it over the base of a shallow glass bowl of approximately 3½ pints/8¾ cups (2 litres) capacity, or divide the cake between individual glass dishes. Squeeze the juice of 2½ oranges over the sponge. Crush 10 oz (275 g) of the raspberries lightly with a fork and spread them over the sponge.

To make the custard, first beat the whole egg and the extra egg yolk with the caster sugar in the top part of a double-boiler. Gradually blend in the scalded single cream, then stir the mixture over barely simmering water until it thickens to the consistency of double cream—this may take 10 minutes. Cool the custard a little before pouring it over the raspberries. When cold, cover and chill for several hours.

The raspberry syllabub topping is best spooned over the trifle close to the time of serving, but the first steps in preparing the syllabub can be, indeed should be, done well ahead. Sieve 6 oz (175 g) of the raspberries to extract the seeds. Sweeten the purée with the icing sugar, flavour it with 1 scant tbsp rose water, and a generous 1 tbsp each of freshly squeezed orange and lemon juice. Cover and leave in a cool place for at least 1 hour to develop full fragrance.

Slowly pour the double cream on to the raspberry purée, beating the purée with a balloon whisk as you do so. Continue beating until the mixture holds a soft shape. Spoon the rich pink syllabub over the trifle and pile the remaining ¼ lb (125 g) raspberries on top. Decorate with a circle of fresh blue borage flowers or crystallised violets if you wish.
SERVES 8 OR MORE

CARDINAL'S COMPOTE

The word cardinal is sometimes used in a culinary context to indicate that a dish includes a raspberry purée; the colour of the purée is thought similar to that of a cardinal's robes. Peaches are a favourite fruit for the cardinal treatment. Melon is less usual but even better I think, particularly if a fragrant variety is used—but even the humble honeydew melon will take on fresh appeal and a hint of glamour if presented at table in this special way. It goes without saying that the success of the dish depends on using fresh ripe berries and a perfectly ripe melon.

1 perfectly ripe Ogen or Charentais melon
a little caster (superfine) sugar
1 lemon
1½ lb (700 g) raspberries
a little icing (confectioners') sugar

Halve the melon and scoop out the seeds. Cut the melon flesh into thin crescent moon slices and trim away the peel.

Dissolve 1 tbsp of caster sugar in a little boiling water and let the mixture cool a little before stirring in the juice of the lemon. Taste and add a little more sugar is necessary—again dissolving the sugar in hot water; the syrup should be sharp but not too acid.

Lay the melon slices in a shallow dish, pour the cold lemon syrup over them, cover and leave to macerate at cool room temperature for 1–2 hours.

Meanwhile rub ½ lb (250 g) of the raspberries through a fine sieve to extract seeds, and sweeten the purée with 1½–2 tbsp icing sugar. Set aside for an hour or so to let the flavour "ripen". Cool room temperature is best—refrigeration would chill and numb the flavours too much.

Shortly before serving, carefully lift the melon slices out of the lemon syrup (save the syrup for a special drink—cook's perks) and arrange them prettily down the centre of a decorative plate—I use a large oval meat dish bought for a song from a junk shop. Scatter the whole raspberries in lines either side of the melon and sift the merest whisper of caster sugar over them if you wish.

Finally, spoon the fresh raspberry sauce down the centre of the melon slices creating a ribbon effect, and serve without delay. Don't be tempted to offer cream with this compôte: it is the combination of sunny fruit flavours that makes it so good.
SERVES 6

COOK'S NOTEBOOK

In winter the conservatory is so cold it doubles as a larder. In spring it slowly sops up tepid warmth from a watery sun. We lunch there, holding our soup spoons in mittened hands, telling ourselves that summer will come. Gradually, over the weeks, we roll up our sleeves and open the windows one by one. In time we not only lunch there but sup and breakfast too. Then, eventually, the day comes when we fling open the doors and, like butterflies emerging from the chrysalis, we break out into the garden.

A garden is a good place for large family gatherings and other parties. In winter we can end up treading on each other's toes, metaphorically and literally, as we huddle round the fire. In the garden there is plenty of breathing space, making it easier to be together and to peel off in ones and twos when we wish.

The best meals in the garden reflect this relaxed and unhurried mood. Lunch, whether it be a self-help buffet, barbecue or sitting round a table, may drift on until teatime, or perhaps even until the onslaught of a mosquitoey dusk drives us indoors. Drinks are just as important as food. The clink of ice in frosted glasses is an archetypal British summer sound.

Some people would argue that *Pimms* is the number-one summer drink, and it certainly looks the part with its pretty flotilla of ice, borage and cucumber. More romantic and quintessentially English, is *elderflower champagne*, surely the queen of the traditional country wines.

I've never made elderflower champagne—or, for that matter, parsley or parsnip or cowslip wine—but I've always rather liked the idea of having my own still room. Not still as in peace and quiet, although it surely should be that, but still as in distil. For it was here, in earlier centuries, that all the lotions, potions and cordials a household needed were brewed and distilled. It was the place where flower waters and other flavourings, pot-pourri, scents, herbal remedies and medicines, tonics and drinks of all sorts, jams, pickles and sweetmeats were made and stored.

Real lemonade (include plenty of lemon zest for a refreshing zing) is so easy to make and so wonderfully thirst-quenching. *Lemon Barley Water* is another favourite—I allow 2 oz/generous $\frac{1}{3}$ cup (50 g) sugar, twice as much barley (pearl or barley flake) and 4 lemons to 2 pints/5 cups (1 litre) water.

Raspberry Cordial—essentially sweetened raspberry vinegar—is another excellent summer drink and it is equally good served hot in winter. Dilute it with boiling water and sip it as the Victorians did to soothe sore throats and to ward off colds. *Raspberry Vinegar* is enjoying vogue status, highly rated by chefs and foodies because of its remarkable fresh fruity fragrance. To make it, put raspberries and vinegar into a large china bowl, allowing 1 lb (450 g) ripe fruit for every 1 pint/ $2\frac{1}{2}$ cups (600 ml) vinegar. Malt is traditional but wine or cider vinegar is more to our taste today. Cover with a cloth and leave in a sunny spot (or in an airing cupboard or close to the kitchen stove if the summer weather plays truant) for 5–7 days, just stirring occasionally. Strain off the liquid, and if you want sensationally fruity results repeat the process using fresh berries. Then bottle the vinegar, label it prettily —and impressive Christmas presents are yours for the giving.

To make *Raspberry Cordial*, add 1 lb/scant $2\frac{1}{2}$ cups (450 g) sugar to each 1 pint/$2\frac{1}{2}$ cups (600 ml) strained fruity vinegar and boil for 10 minutes before bottling.

Raspberries make wonderful jam but strawberry jam is best of all—or can be if it contains lots of tiny heart-shaped fruit prettily suspended in a glowing jelly preserve. Strawberries are notoriously poor setters, prolonged cooking ruins flavour and colour, and all that business with sugar thermometers and doing saucer tests can be a bit nerve-racking. I've given up. Or, rather, I've been won over by the modern freezer method of jam-making.

Call it cheating if you like, but I think it makes sense—and the proof is in the eating. Open a pot of best *Strawberry Jam* in midwinter and you recapture vividly the true taste of summer. Layer in a large china bowl 3 lb (1.4 kg) small, perfectly sound, slightly under-ripe strawberries and 4 lb (1.8 kg) sugar, lightly crushing the berries into the sugar as you layer them. Leave at room temperature until the sugar has fully dissolved. This may take a couple of hours. Add 8 fl oz/scant 1 cup (200 ml) liquid pectin and stir vigorously for 3 minutes then pot the fruity mixture into small freezerproof containers. Leave in a cool place for 24 hours then cover, label and freeze (for up to seven months). Store in the fridge after defrosting. To make *Raspberry and Redcurrant Jam*, simply replace the strawberries with a mixture of these two fruits.

RED AND WHITE VELVET

In this handsome and luxurious dish a beautifully fresh fruit salad is teamed with a velvet-textured mousse. For extra panache, sprigs of Philadelphus (mock orange blossom) can be arranged around the base of the mousse after unmoulding. This looks charming and the scent is wonderful, prettily echoing the flavouring used in the mousse.

1½ tbsp gelatine powder
2 large eggs and 2 oz/generous ⅓ cup (50 g) caster (superfine) sugar
½ pint/1¼ cups (300 ml) Greek ewes' milk yoghurt
2 tbsp triple distilled orange blossom water
½ pint/1¼ cups (300 ml) double (heavy) cream

For the compôte:
about ¾ lb (350 g) each: strawberries, raspberries (or loganberries), cherries and redcurrants
a spoonful or two of caster sugar
2 small oranges and 1 lemon

Sprinkle the gelatine powder on to 4 tbsp cold water in a small pan and leave to soften and swell. Separate the eggs. Beat the yolks and sugar with an electric whisk until the mixture falls in ribbons, then beat in the yoghurt. Dissolve the gelatine over low heat and set it aside to cool. Meanwhile whisk the egg whites to shiny peaks; add the orange blossom water to the cream and whip softly; select a kugelhopf or ring mould of 2½ pint/6¼ cup (1.4 litre) capacity and rinse it out with very cold water.

Beat the cooling gelatine into the egg yolk and yoghurt mixture. Quickly fold in the cream, then the egg whites, and turn the mixture into the mould. Work swiftly as the mixture begins to set very rapidly. Cover and chill the velvety rich mousse for several hours.

Stone the cherries, string the redcurrants and hull the raspberries or loganberries. Hull the strawberries and halve or quarter them depending on size. Pile the fruit into a bowl, sprinkling a little sugar between layers. Pour on the freshly squeezed citrus juice, toss gently and cover. Leave at cool room temperature (do not refrigerate) for half an hour or more, during which time the red fruit juices will mingle deliciously with the sugar and citrus to make a light fruity syrup.

Unmould the mousse shortly before serving and pile some of the fruit into the centre. Serve the rest of the compôte in a bowl, handing it round separately so that everyone can help themselves.
SERVES 8–10

QUEEN OF JELLIES

An aptly named jelly—brilliantly coloured and with a wonderful pure fruity flavour. A garnish of frosted redcurrants provides the perfect finishing touch. If you are nervous about unmoulding, make and serve the jelly in glasses instead. It looks just as pretty and needs less gelatine powder—2 scant tbsp—which allows the redcurrant taste to shine through even better.

For the jelly:
1¼ lb (600 g) redcurrants
6 oz/scant 1 cup (175 g) caster (superfine) sugar
1 pint/2½ cups (600 ml) warm water
2 slightly rounded tbsp gelatine powder

For the frosted redcurrants:
caster sugar
1 egg white
½ lb (225 g) redcurrants

To make the jelly, put the redcurrants into a saucepan (there is no need to string them). Add the sugar and warm water. Cover and cook gently over low heat until the fruit is perfectly tender.

Tip the contents of the pan into a sieve placed over a bowl. Crush the fruit lightly with a potato masher, then leave until the juices have dripped into the bowl.

Measure 6 tbsp boiling water into a separate bowl. Sprinkle on the gelatine powder and whisk briskly with a fork until the gelatine has dissolved to a perfectly clear liquid. Pour on the warm redcurrant juices, whisking the gelatine mixture all the time as you pour. Measure the combined liquids and top up with cold water as necessary to make a total of 2 pints/5 cups (1 litre). Pour the jelly into a mould which has been rinsed out with cold water, and leave in a cold place to set.

To make frosted redcurrants, first beat the egg white with a fork in a soup plate—just enough to make the egg white smooth and very runny, not frothy. Sprinkle the work surface with sugar and cover a large rack with greaseproof paper. Holding a branch of redcurrants by the stalk, dip the fruit into the egg white. Gently shake off excess egg, then sweep the branch to and fro across the work surface to dust it with sugar. Coat the remaining branches of fruit in the same way and lay them in a single layer on the rack to dry. Within 30 minutes or so the frosting will have set to a crust.

Unmould the jelly shortly before serving, and arrange the frosted redcurrants in a garland around the base.
SERVES 8

BACK TO FRONT: QUEEN OF JELLIES, RED AND WHITE VELVET

FRESH RASPBERRY BAKEWELL

This version of Bakewell Tart, or Bakewell Pudding as it used to be called in its native Derbyshire, is more expensive than most, but I think you will agree it tastes better than most. What makes it special is the lavish use of fresh fruit, instead of the usual smear of jam, and the inclusion of freshly-ground almonds. Cake crumbs steeped in almond essence (frequently just a chemical compound) are no substitute for ground almonds, and almonds that are freshly ground at home have a very superior flavour to ageing shop-bought ground almonds.

¼ lb/1 stick (125 g) butter, or lard and butter mixed
¼ lb/scant 1 cup (125 g) plain (all-purpose) flour
¼ lb/scant 1 cup (125 g) plain wholemeal (whole wheat) flour

For the filling:
¼ lb/1 stick (125 g) butter
¼ lb/generous ½ cup (125 g) caster (superfine) sugar
¼ lb/scant 1 cup (125 g) shelled almonds
½ tsp triple distilled rose water
2 large eggs
¾ lb (350 g) firm fresh raspberries or loganberries

Cut then rub the fat into the flours and bind the dough with about 8 tsp cold water. Use the pastry to line a 10 inch (25 cm) fluted flan tin with removable base. Completely blind bake the pastry case and let it become cold.

Hull and thoroughly chill the berries. Drop the nuts into a pan of boiling water and leave for a minute or so to loosen their skins. Slip off the skins and grind the nuts to a powder. Everything up to this stage can be done several hours ahead.

Heat the oven to 400°F (200°C), mark 6. Dice the butter and barely melt it in a small saucepan over low heat. Away from the heat, add the sugar then stir in the ground almonds, the rose water and the lightly beaten eggs, in that order. Tip the chilled berries into the prebaked pastry case, spreading them evenly, and pour the almond mixture over the fruit. Bake for 35–40 minutes until the Bakewell topping is pale gold and puffed up.

Although this delicious pudding can be eaten cold, it is best served warm (not piping hot), lightly dusted with icing sugar and accompanied by a bowl of chilled cream, yoghurt or fromage blanc.
SERVES 6–8

HOT RASPBERRY AND REDCURRANT TARTS

Cooking raspberries just long enough to make them warm heightens their fragrance beautifully and these tarts make a lovely choice of pudding for a cool day. They are surprisingly filling. The finishing touches and final cooking must be done immediately before serving, so this recipe is better suited to relaxed and informal occasions than to grand entertaining.

5 oz/1¼ sticks (150 g) butter
10 oz/2 cups (300 g) plain (all-purpose) flour
the finely grated zest of 1 small orange
2½ tbsp freshly-squeezed orange juice
1 lb 2 oz (500 g) raspberries
generous ½ lb (250 g) redcurrants
3 oz/scant ½ cup (75 g) vanilla sugar

Cut then rub the butter into the sifted flour. Stir in the orange zest and bind the dough with the orange juice. Knead the pastry lightly, roll it out and use it to line six 4–4½ inch (11 cm) individual fluted tart tins with removable bases.

Line the pastry shells with greaseproof paper and weigh down with baking beans. Blind bake on a preheated baking sheet for 15 minutes at 400°F (200°C), mark 6. Remove lining paper and beans and bake the pastry for a further 15 minutes until pale golden and crisp. Cool the tarts completely before wrapping and storing them in an airtight tin. (Keep the tarts in their tins to protect the pastry against breakage.)

Shortly before serving, unwrap the tarts and slide them out of their tins on to a baking sheet. Put the baking sheet into an oven heated to 350°F (180°C), mark 4 and leave for 10 minutes or so until the pastry is hot. Sprinkle the raspberries and redcurrants with the vanilla sugar and toss gently to mix. Pile the fruit into the pastry shells and cook for 7–8 minutes only. The idea is to make the fruit warm and aromatic, not to cook it until squashy and flowing with juices. Use a fish slice to transfer the tarts to very hot pudding plates and serve immediately—with softly whipped cream, fromage blanc, or yoghurt if you wish.
SERVES 6

TAVERNER'S CHERRIES

Stoning cherries is a tiresome business, unless you use one of those special little stoning gadgets, which does the job very neatly and speeds up the task considerably. Take care, however, not to splash your clothes with spurts of cherry juice—it can stain badly. Take care too not to over-cook cherries or their flavour and shape will be spoiled and the lovely rich colour will be weakened. Kirsch is the natural choice of liqueur to use for this dish since it is of course made from cherry stone kernels, but white rum makes a pleasant alternative.

2 lb (900 g) dark red dessert cherries
½ lb/generous 1 cup (225 g) granulated sugar
the finely pared peel of 1 large orange and 1 lemon
8 tbsp kirsch
¾ pint/scant 2 cups (425 ml) each Greek strained yoghurt
   and ewes' milk yoghurt (or equal quantities of
   yoghurt and fromage blanc if preferred)

Stone the cherries. Put the sugar into a saucepan; add the citrus peel, kirsch and 1 pint/2½ cups (575 ml) water. Bring to the boil as slowly as possible. Add the cherries, bring back to the boil and simmer gently for 3–4 minutes only.

Draw the pan away from the heat, cover and leave until completely cold, by which time the cherries will be perfectly tender but still holding their shape nicely. Lift out the cherries with a slotted spoon and put them into a bowl.

Fast boil the cherry liquid until reduced to 6 fl oz/ ¾ cup (175 ml) of sticky rich syrup. Strain to extract the peel and pour the syrup over the cherries. Cover and set aside in a cold larder for several hours (or up to 48 hours) just turning the fruit occasionally.

To serve, spoon the yoghurt into a pretty bowl. Or, better still, divide the yoghurt between 8 glasses. Add the yoghurt in soft spoonfuls, don't pack it tightly, then pile the cherries and their syrup on top. The idea is that the syrup should gently ooze its way down into little airpockets in the yoghurt, creating streaks of rich colour and aromatic sweetness. Serve within an hour or so of making these finishing touches, and accompany the pudding with miniature macaroons if wished.
SERVES 8

SECRET STRAWBERRY MOUSSE

Whereas most sweet mousses are choc-a-bloc with cholesterol-rich eggs and cream, this one is beautifully light and unusually fruity in flavour. Including a banana helps to keep costs down and increases the fibre value of the dish. No one will taste the banana provided you use a small one. If proportions are altered, the cook's secret will be out.

1 lb (450 g) strawberries
½ pint/1¼ cups (275 ml) strawberry yoghurt
1 very small, very ripe banana
the zest of half a small orange
caster (superfine) sugar and gelatine powder
1 large egg white

Sieve a few of the strawberries into a small bowl and reserve for garnishing the mouse. Similarly, set aside (in a separate small bowl) 2 or 3 tbsp of the yoghurt.

Chop the banana and process it in a blender or food processor together with the remaining strawberries, the orange zest and 3 tbsp sugar. Add the ingredients gradually, stopping the machine and pushing the fruit firmly down on to the blades as necessary to produce a perfectly smooth pink purée. Add the yoghurt and process again briefly to mix well. Sieve the mixture to extract seeds if you wish.

Sprinkle 4 tsp gelatine powder on to 3 tbsp boiling water and stir vigorously with a fork until the gelatine has dissolved to a clear liquid. Cool slightly before thoroughly beating the gelatine into the strawberry mixture. Cover and refrigerate the mixture until it is syrupy thick.

Whisk the egg white to snowy peaks and fold it into the syrupy thick mousse mixture. Turn the mousse into a 2 pint/5 cup (1 litre approx.) serving dish. Drizzle the reserved strawberry purée over the top and swirl it with the tip of a skewer to create a marbled effect, then do the same thing with the reserved yoghurt. Cover the mousse and chill it until set firm.

Bring back to room temperature about 1 hour before serving. If too cold the fresh fruity flavours will be numbed. I think it is quite unnecessary, indeed undesirable, to accompany the mouse with cream or yoghurt.

SERVES 4–5

WILD STRAWBERRY BLANCMANGE

This beautifully simple yet sophisticated confection bears no resemblance whatsoever to the stodgy and tasteless object that used to be served up in the name of blancmange in schools and other institutions, and was generally known as "white shape" by the inmates. Creamy, yet not over-rich, delicately flavoured and set to the softest of jellies, this slips down the throat silkily. It makes a beautiful finale for a special-occasion dinner, but take care not to precede it with very pungent foods, or the subtle taste of the blancmange will be overpowered.

2½ tsp gelatine powder
1 pint/2½ cups (575 ml) semi-skimmed milk
2½ oz/scant ⅓ cup (65 g) caster (superfine) sugar
¼ pint/⅔ cup (150 ml) half cream
¼ pint/⅔ cup (150 ml) single (light) cream
¼ pint/⅔ cup (150 ml) scant 3 tbsp framboise or white rum
a few Alpine or wood strawberries

Measure 3 tbsp cold water into a cup. Sprinkle on the gelatine powder and leave to soak for 5 minutes. Meanwhile put half the milk into a small pan, add the sugar and warm over low heat just long enough to melt the sugar. Set the milkpan aside.

Stand the cup of soaked gelatine in a bowl of hot water and stir until the gelatine dissolves to a clear liquid. Pour the mixture on to the warm milk in a slow trickle, stirring the milk all the while, then "wash out" the cup by pouring some of the milk back and forth between cup and milkpan.

Carefully stir the remaining (cold) milk into the pan, then add both types of cream, and finally the framboise or white rum. Pour the mixture into small pretty glasses and leave in a cold larder until the blancmange has set to a delicate trembling creamy jelly.

Carefully lay a few Alpine or wood strawberries on top of each pudding just before serving, and garland the plates with a few wild strawberry flowers and leaves. Only a few wild strawberries are needed to crown the blancmange. If none are available, use ordinary strawberries—small ones. Slice them thinly and dust them lightly with lemon sugar. To make this, rub sugar cubes against the skin of a lemon and crush to a powder.

SERVES 6

LEFT TO RIGHT: SECRET STRAWBERRY MOUSSE, WILD STRAWBERRY BLANCMANGE

Cool Food

When a summer's day lives up to its name, I want to spend as much time as possible outside and very little in the kitchen. I mind about good food as much as ever. I am quite happy to do things like topping and tailing beans and making mayonnaise: they are agreeable and soothing little tasks, which can be easily done as I sit in sun-dappled shade in the garden. What I resent is the thought of hot hours slaving over the stove. I'm sure most cooks feel the same way, sharing my view that the cook needs and deserves time off every bit as much as the rest of the family.

It is in fact unnecessary for the cook to spend long hours cooped up in the kitchen on high summer days. After all, no one is ravenously hungry when the weather is hot: what little cooking needs to be done can often be done in the cool of the evening; and most of us these days are lucky enough to have blenders or food processors to help make fast, light work of the worst of the chores.

In winter the body needs food as fuel. As the sun grows stronger in summer, appetites flag and the cook's role changes accordingly. Instead of satisfying basic hunger she now needs to tempt and entice family and friends to take the nourishment and refreshment they need. A light hand is essential. Blanket-thick sauces spell suffocation and the lavish use of butter, cream or oil seems horribly sickly. Rich and heavy foods are out. So are elaborate and tricksy presentations. Plates cluttered with fussy foods make one feel disagreeably hot and bothered just to look at them. To put it bluntly, it's a waste of time to labour like Hercules when simplicity wins.

The foods that give most pleasure on very hot days are essentially pure and simple. Think of pastel pale soup served in small cups, beautifully chilled, agreeably thin and delicately creamy. Think of cool, perfectly crisp salad leaves, sprinkled with a few green herbs, a squeeze of lemon and a drop of best olive oil. Think of sunny ripe nectarines and figs, just one each, thoughtfully peeled and partially cut into segments for lazy eating, prettily laid out on a plate. Foods like these are a joy because they are elegant, light, crisp and juicy.

In high summer feelings of thirst are far stronger than hunger, so the moistness of food assumes special importance. Iced soups are ideal heatwave food (food and drink neatly combined in one) and

salads and fruits rate highly: the fact that fruit and vegetables are largely composed of water is what gives them the edge over more solid foods. Many meats and fish can seem just too heavy, too dry in very hot weather. How much more appealing, how much more easily they slip down the throat if chopped or flaked and generously anointed with a cool dressing or bathed in a light mousse mixture.

Quantities are important: keep them small. Too much, however good, can seem daunting. It is crucial, too, to serve foods at the right temperature. Foods that have lost their cool are very unappetising. No one wants to eat cricket-match sandwiches prepared hours ahead and left unprotected in the warm so the ham turns to leather and the bread curls away from it with stale disdain.

Chilled soups should be really cold. Serve them more or less straight from the fridge, in soup cups or plates that have also been chilled. If there is room, I put soup cups into the fridge. Otherwise, I fill them with ice-cubes, or stand them, together with other crockery needed for the meal, in a sink filled with icy water. But remember to empty and dry soup cups just before serving. To serve soup with ice floating in it is a mistake: ice can cause curdling and melts leaving tasteless watery pools in its wake.

Be firm with mousses and jellies in very hot weather. Prevent them collapsing in a shame-faced way by erring on the generous side when measuring out the gelatine powder. Unmould—if the recipe calls for unmoulding—close to mealtime. If there has to be a delay between unmoulding the mousse or jelly on to a plate and serving, cover it with the inverted mould and store in the cool of the fridge or a proper old-fashioned north-facing larder until needed. Take particular care with dishes containing fatty ingredients. Foods coated with cream or mayonnaise-based sauces sweat easily and butter turns rancid in the heat.

It is best to serve food from indoors, encouraging everyone to help themselves, to carry their plates and glasses outdoors for eating, and to come back in for refills. If you insist on doing the serving out in the garden be sure to place your "sideboard" in a shady spot. It makes sense, and looks pretty, to set each serving dish on a larger one which has been packed with ice-cubes to provide an aura of cool.

Handsome presentation makes all the difference to our enjoyment of food—after all we eat with our eyes even before we taste food—and making foods look as good as they taste is one of the pleasures of cooking. Fancy twirls of piped cream, radish roses and the like are my pet hates and I dislike them more than ever in hot weather, when the eye is easily tired by fussy shapes. Cool clean lines are much more appetising and the natural look wins over the contrived every time. Food looks deliciously simple if it is neatly piled, rustic fashion, on dishes lined with fresh green cabbage leaves; the living green of the leaves somehow seems to intensify the fresh look of the food. A meat, fish or rice salad can look spectacular served in the scooped-out shell of a huge tiger-striped yellow and green marrow or an orangey pink pumpkin. This is a practical suggestion, not a decorative ploy. The thick-walled vegetable shell provides cool insulation and the scooped-out flesh need not be wasted: use it to make jam or chutney. Topping or circling food with a garland of flowers or herbs makes a charming finishing touch and can provide a useful indication of the flavourings used in cooking the dish.

Soup is everyone's favourite lunchtime food in winter, but the idea of lunching on soup in summer seems relatively unusual. I can't think why. Nothing seems to me more welcome on a hot summer's day than good chilled soup: such elegant and light sustenance is more or less guaranteed to refresh my heat-jaded palate when most other foods seem just too substantial. In winter we usually serve lunch-time soup with great hunks of bread and cheese on the side. That seems much too hefty now—unless the weather plays foul. But a little lunch of summery soup can be delightfully rounded off by a delicate nibble of bread. A single nanny-thin slice of fresh home-baked bread and unsalted butter could be just the answer. It is appropriately small: there is enough of the child in us all to enjoy having it cut into "soldiers" or small triangles; and it suits our lazy mood to have it ready prepared and handed to us on a plate. Miniature sandwiches are also appealing, particularly open sandwiches. I don't mean anything as high-rise or as ornate as *smørrebrød* but good honest English sandwiches that have, so to speak, discarded their top layer of bread to show off their filling and to make lighter eating. I like to use a variety of breads—granary, rye, saffron, rice, herb and soda as well as wholemeal (pages 30–41)—and I like to ring the changes sometimes by spreading the bread with something other than butter. Here are some particularly good combinations:

◇ Wholemeal bread spread with curd cheese, topped with finely chopped sorrel
◇ Rye bread spread with scrambled eggs, creamily bound with a little mayonnaise, topped with a tuft of mustard and cress
◇ Rice bread lightly spread with yeast extract or peanut butter, topped with cucumber
◇ Granary bread spread with butter, studded with walnuts and sprinkled with salt
◇ Brown bread and butter, topped with the thinnest possible slices of orange
◇ White bread spread with anchovy paste, topped with a little bouquet of fresh dill

COOL CUCUMBER SOUP

Laced with tender shreds of cucumber flesh, and subtly tinted with cucumber peel, this seems to me a particularly good cucumber soup. And, as good fortune would have it, it is very quick and easy to make.

1 large cucumber
half a stock cube (1 boullion cube)— chicken, fish or vegetable
tarragon or white wine vinegar
caster(superfine) sugar
fresh dill
¾ pint/scant 2 cups (450 ml) thick creamy home-made yoghurt or 1 × 480 g tub Greek strained yoghurt

Peel the cucumber, halve it and scoop out the seeds. Discard the seeds and reserve the peel. Cut the flesh into fine shreds, either cutting them by hand into little pieces no larger than matchsticks, or (much quicker and just as pretty) by using the coarse grater blade of a food processor.

Dissolve the stock cube in 150 ml (¼ pint/⅔ cup) boiling water. Stir in 1½ tsp vinegar, 1 tsp caster sugar and ½ tsp salt.

Put the stock into a food processor, add the cucumber peel and process until you have a green-flecked purée. Stop and start the machine several times and push the cucumber peel down on to the blades in order to chop it as finely as possible. Strain the liquid through a sieve, pressing the tiny shreds of cucumber peel with a wooden spoon to extract every drop of green liquid from it.

Stir the green liquid into a few spoonfuls of the yoghurt, then stir this mixture into the rest of the yoghurt, slowly and gently to make a perfectly smooth, very pale green cream. Then stir in the finely shredded cucumber flesh and 1–2 tbsp coarsely chopped dill—include the very finely chopped stalks as well as the feathery leaves as they are rich in flavour.

Cover and chill for several hours before serving to allow flavours to infuse. Check seasoning, thin to taste with a little iced water or stock if you wish, and serve in chilled soup plates or cups, garnished with small fronds of fresh dill. Granary or rye bread makes an excellent accompaniment to this delicious and pretty pale green soup.
SERVES 4

LEFT TO RIGHT: TOASTED ALMOND AND WATERCRESS SOUP (PAGE 66), CREAMY FISH SOUP WITH FENNEL (PAGE 66)

TOASTED ALMOND AND WATERCRESS SOUP

Watercress soups are usually peppery and clean-tasting. Some are sharpened with buttermilk. Some are thickened and softened with potato. Many include onion. This one, more surprisingly, is enriched with the nutty sweetness of well toasted and very finely ground almonds. The result is attractive and soothing.

5 or 6 large bunches of watercress
generous 2 pints/5 cups (1 litre) good home-made stock,
    preferably chicken stock
3 oz/scant ¾ cup (75 g) flaked almonds
2 × 480 g tubs Greek strained yoghurt

Wash the watercress and shake it dry. Snip off and discard any very tough hairy stalks and yellowing leaves. Chop the good parts roughly or simply break each stem into two shorter lengths.

Put the watercress into a saucepan and add the chicken stock, which should be cold. Bring to the boil, reduce heat to a bare simmer, cover and leave to cook gently for about 8 minutes. Meanwhile toast the almonds under the grill. Toast them slowly and gently until deep gold in colour all over and intensely nutty in flavour.

Reduce the toasted nuts to a fine powder, preferably using an electric coffee mill or spice mill. A food processor or blender can be used, but you will have to stop and start the machine many times over, and push the nuts well down onto the blades, or some will be very finely ground and the rest only broken into small chips.

Using a slotted spoon, transfer the cooked watercress from the saucepan to a food processor or blender and reduce to a very fine, green-flecked, purée. Add the powdered nuts and process again. Add the yoghurt and process for a third time. Then, keeping the machine running, gradually pour on and blend in the hot watercress-flavoured stock. Season the soup well with salt and pepper and set it aside to cool.

Cover and refrigerate for several hours. Serve well chilled, garnished with a few flaked and toasted almonds and a sprig or two of watercress. The nutty sweetness of the almonds seems to give this soup a certain warmth and roundness of flavour, which is very attractive in itself and makes the soup particularly welcome on days when the sun is not shining quite as brightly as it might be.
SERVES 8–10

CREAMY FISH SOUP WITH FENNEL

Although this soup takes a bit more time and effort to prepare, there is something very pleasing about using the shells of the prawns instead of just throwing them away. The result is a refreshing and sophisticated soup with an excellent shellfish flavour.

1 lb (450 g) cooked prawns (shrimp) in the shell
1 lb (450 g) coley or other white fish fillets
1 large bulb Florentine fennel
1 lemon
coriander seeds, anchovy essence (extract) and cornflour
    (cornstarch)
¼ pint/⅔ cup (150 ml) semi-skimmed milk
2½ fl oz/generous ⅓ cup (60 ml) soured cream

Shell the prawns and put the shells into a large saucepan. Add the fillets of fish and the finely chopped fennel, saving the fennel fronds to garnish the soup. Add the juice of half a lemon, 1 tsp coriander seeds bruised with mortar and pestle, and a few peppercorns.

Pour on 2½ pints/6¼ cups (1.4 litres) cold water, bring slowly to simmering point, cover and simmer for 25 minutes to make a richly flavoured fish stock. Strain the stock: tip the contents of the pan into a sieve placed over a deep bowl and press the debris in the sieve with a potato masher to encourage trapped juices to drip through. Check and adjust seasoning to taste.

Put almost all the peeled prawns into a food processor and whizz until chopped very finely indeed. Add the juice of the remaining half lemon and a generous shake of anchovy essence and whizz again to make the mixture as smooth as possible.

Put the prawn purée into a saucepan; gradually stir in the fish stock and warm over gentle heat for 3–4 minutes, stirring continuously. Stir in 3 tbsp cornflour, mixed to a paste with a little cold water. Simmer for 1–2 minutes, stirring all the time, to thicken the soup a little. Then rub the soup through a sieve or (easier and every bit as effective) pass it through the finest blade of a Mouli-légumes. Blend the milk and soured cream together until quite smooth, then stir in. Check seasoning and chill the soup very thoroughly indeed. Thin to taste further, if you wish, just before serving, and garnish with fennel fronds and reserved whole prawns.
SERVES 6–8

PEACHY RICE SALAD

This is the sort of dish that tempts me to turn vegetarian, as the combination of textures and tastes is so appealing. It's a lovely salad to serve on a very hot day when everyone is in happy holiday mood. It needs no accompaniments except good bread and nothing need precede or follow it. But if you want to serve something afterwards I suggest not a pudding or fruit but a simple lettuce and cucumber salad, topped with snowy spoonfuls of fromage blanc or slivers of ripe, creamy Brie.

½ lb/1⅓ cups (250 g) brown rice
2 oranges and 2 lemons
garlic, coriander seeds, rosemary, oregano and fresh
  thyme, preferably lemon thyme
½ lb (250 g) each runner and French beans
½ lb (250 g) each broad (fava) beans and young peas,
  shelled weights
¼ lb (125 g) each shelled walnuts, hazelnuts, pumpkin
  seeds and sunflower seeds
8 perfectly ripe peaches, or 2 lb (1 kg) grapes
8 tbsp Greek strained yoghurt or fromage blanc

Cook the rice, together with the zest of the oranges, in double its volume of water. When just cooked, tip it into a large bowl and season it very highly indeed. I use 3 fat garlic cloves crushed with plenty of salt, 3–4 tsp coriander seeds and 1 tsp dried rosemary pounded with mortar and pestle, lots of pepper, 4–5 tsp fresh lemon thyme (or a smaller amount of ordinary thyme plus lemon zest) and some oregano.

Cook the vegetables until just tender and add them, as soon as cooked, to the rice bowl. Mix well, allow to become cold then chill.

Toast the nuts and seeds in a dry frying pan over low heat until aromatic, and reserve.

Skin and stone the peaches, cut the flesh into thin crescent moon slices and toss gently in the juice of 1 orange and half a lemon. If you can't get very ripe peaches use grapes instead: halve and pip them.

Close to serving time, blend the juice of 1 orange and half a lemon into the yoghurt or fromage blanc, then stir in the juices that have collected in the bowl of peaches or grapes. Pour this mixture into the rice bowl and toss well. Add the prepared fruit and nuts and mix in gently. Add extra lemon juice, herbs and other seasonings to taste and serve garnished with herbs. Do not assemble the salad ahead of serving as it loses its freshness surprisingly quickly.

SERVES 8–10

DEVILISH CHICKEN SALAD

The idea of dressing poultry and fruit with a very mildly devilled sauce is ancient but it seems much less commonplace today than a curry cream sauce. For delightful effect, serve this delicious salad in a rustic manner, piling it into the scooped-out shell of a marrow or pumpkin and adding an edible garland of flowers.

3½–4 lb (1.6–1.8 kg) free-range, corn-fed or poulet noir
  chicken
2 lemons, tarragon, bay, coriander seeds
1 egg yolk and ¼ pint/⅔ cup (150 ml) vegetable oil
Worcestershire sauce and tomato ketchup
5 tbsp Greek ewe's milk yoghurt
fresh mint
2 oz/scant ⅓ cup (50 g) cashew nuts
3 large, perfectly ripe mangoes or 4 or 5 dessert pears or
  a large perfectly ripe melon
½ lb/4 cups (225 g) small cap mushrooms
pot marigolds and/or nasturtium flowers (optional)

Poach the chicken a day ahead, cooking it in enough water to cover the thickest part of the thigh meat, and include lemon, tarragon, bay and coriander seeds in the pot for flavouring.

To make the sauce, carefully beat the oil into the egg yolk as though making mayonnaise. Then gradually stir in 1½–2 tbsp Worcestershire sauce, 1–1½ tsp tomato ketchup and the yoghurt. Add salt to taste and a dash more Worcestershire sauce or a touch of mustard if you like. Aim for a mildly devilled sauce that is smooth and thick— don't make it too runny.

Skin and bone the cold cooked chicken, cut or pull the flesh into generous bite-size pieces and add it to the sauce. Toss gently, adding 1–2 tbsp fresh mint leaves, cover and set aside in a cool place for at least 1 hour.

Toast the nuts and reserve them. Peel and cube the fruit, sprinkle with lemon juice and reserve separately. Slice the mushrooms, season with salt, pepper and lemon and reserve in yet another bowl.

Assemble the salad close to serving time. Drain the mushrooms and the fruit from their juices. Add them and the nuts to the chicken and toss gently. Then pile the mixture on to a serving platter or into a large scooped-out marrow or pumpkin shell, scattering mint leaves and nasturtium or pot marigold petals between layers, if available. Serve with plain lettuce and brown soda bread or with a simple rice or burghul wheat salad.

SERVES 6

SMOKED HADDOCK MOUSSE

On a sun-baked day I fill the centre of this fishy mousse with a cool salad of cucumber and water-cress. For a richer and sunnier effect, I fill it with a colourful salad of tomatoes, peppers, French beans, brown rice and black olives. If more people turn up than planned, it is easy enough to stretch the meal at the 11th hour: make extra salad, serving some in the centre of the mousse and more in a bowl.

1 small carrot and 6 or 7 spring onions (scallions)
fennel seeds and a bay leaf
generous ¾ pint/2 cups (450 ml) milk
generous 1 lb (450 g) smoked haddock fillets
1½ oz/3 tbsp (40 g) each butter and plain (all-purpose) flour
1 slightly heaped tbsp gelatine powder
5 tbsp cream or fromage blanc
2 egg whites

Chop the vegetables very finely. Bruise 2 or 3 fennel seeds and half a dozen black peppercorns. Put them into a pan with a bay leaf and the milk and bring to scalding point as slowly as possible to infuse the milk well. Draw the pan away from the heat. Add the fish, pushing it well down into the liquid, and bring back to simmering point. Switch off the heat, cover the pan and leave it for 10 minutes.

Lift out the fish. Discard the bay leaf, pepper-corns and fennel seeds, put the vegetables and the fish-flavoured milk into a blender and whizz to a purée.

Cook the butter and flour to a pale straw-coloured paste and blend in the milky purée to make a rich sauce. Add the fish (skinned, boned and broken into chunks) and simmer without a lid over very low heat for 5–10 minutes, stirring occasionally.

Sprinkle the gelatine powder on to 2 or 3 spoonfuls of cold water in a cup and dissolve over a pan of hot water. Thoroughly stir the hot liquid gelatine into the fish pan. Away from the heat, stir in the cream and season to taste with plenty of pepper, perhaps a little cayenne and a little salt. Turn the mixture into a bowl and set aside until cold and beginning to thicken. Then whisk the egg whites to shiny peaks, fold them into the mousse mixture and turn the mixture into a ring mould or kugelhopf mould which has been rinsed out with cold water. Cover and refrigerate until set firm.

Unmould shortly before serving and fill the centre of the mousse with a pretty and suitable accompanying salad.
SERVES 4–8

PARSONAGE EGG MOUSSE

This pretty mousse, attractively flavoured with herbs, needs good home-made chicken stock to set it. Make it in individual ramekins for an appetiser, or in one big bowl for a lunch dish. I like to accompany the mousse with granary bread and butter and a delicate salad of lettuce hearts scattered with herbs or sprinkled with peas, cucumber and perhaps a few asparagus tips.

fresh tarragon, parsley and chervil
scant 1 pint/2½ cups (550 ml) richly flavoured home-made chicken stock that sets to a soft jelly
6 whole eggs plus 1 egg yolk
¼ pint/⅔ cup (150 ml) olive and sunflower oil, mixed
tarragon vinegar and dry sherry
1 tbsp gelatine powder
1 × 225 g tub Greek ewes' milk yoghurt

Take 4 or 5 large sprigs each of chervil, parsley and tarragon. Bruise them and bring them slowly to simmering point in half (not all) the chicken stock. Set aside to infuse for 30 minutes. Meanwhile, hard-boil the 6 eggs and cool them.

Make a mayonnaise with the egg yolk, the two sorts of oil, 1 tsp tarragon vinegar and some salt and pepper.

Strain the herb-flavoured stock. Sprinkle the gelatine powder into it, leave to soak, then dissolve over gentle heat. Cool slightly, then beat in the rest of the stock and 1 tbsp sherry. Reserve about quarter of this mixture for garnishing the mousse. Carefully and gradually stir the rest into the yoghurt, then gradually blend this combination into the mayonnaise to make a perfectly smooth cream. If it looks at all lumpy, rub it through a sieve. Season and chill the mixture until it becomes syrupy thick, which means it is approaching setting point—1 hour or so.

Peel the hard-boiled eggs and chop them roughly, having reserved a few thin slices to garnish the mousse. Gently but thoroughly mix the chopped eggs into the thickening creamy mousse mixture. Check and adjust seasoning to taste. Put the mixture into a pretty bowl or dish of approximately 2½ pint/6¼ cup (1.4 litre) capacity, cover and chill until just set.

Decorate with the reserved slices of egg and a gar-land of fresh herbs, then carefully spoon on the remaining cool liquid gelatine mixture so the decoration is sealed under a thin layer of delicately flavoured pale amber jelly. Cover the dish with cling film and refrigerate until shortly before serving.
SERVES 4–8

BACK TO FRONT: INDIVIDUAL PARSONAGE EGG MOUSSE, SMOKED HADDOCK MOUSSE

PINK PASTA SALAD

This unusual salad boasts beautifully fresh flavour and colour. The raw tomato sauce is simply whizzed in a blender; the peppers can be raw but are best grilled to make them digestible and mellow tasting. For very special occasions add some snippets of smoked salmon. For a vegetarian feast omit the prawns, use more tomato chunks and herbs and add diced avocado just before serving.

3 large red peppers
virgin olive oil, lemon juice
1½ lb (700 g) tomatoes
garlic
sugar
¾ lb/3 cups (350 g) small pasta shapes, preferably bows
    and corkscrews
a bunch of chives and basil or mint
10–12 oz (300–350 g) cooked and shelled prawns
    (shrimp)

Cook the peppers under the grill (broiler), turning as necessary, until the skins are blistered all over and the flesh feels soft underneath. As soon as the peppers are cool enough to handle, strip away the papery skins, cut away stalk ends and scrape away the seeds. Chop the flesh into chunks and dress with plenty of black pepper, a good squeeze or two of lemon juice and 3 tbsp olive oil.

Skin and seed all the tomatoes. Put half of them into a blender or food processor, add 1–2 crushed garlic cloves, 2 generous pinches of sugar, a good squeeze of lemon juice and 3 tbsp olive oil. Whizz to a smooth purée and season very generously with pepper and some salt. Turn the mixture into a large serving bowl.

Cut the rest of the skinned and seeded tomatoes into chunks and add them with the red peppers and their dressing.

About 30 minutes before you want to serve the salad, boil the pasta. Drain it thoroughly and add it, while still hot, to the bowl of tomatoes and peppers. Toss gently to mix everything and to encourage the pasta to absorb the delicious flavourings of the vegetables and their dressing.

Set the bowl aside for about 20 minutes until the mixture is cool but not cold. Then add the peeled prawns and some fresh, chopped herbs. I suggest at least 3 or 4 tbsp of freshly snipped chives and the leaves of several sprigs of basil or mint. Basil and mint leaves are best simply torn to little pieces with the fingers, not chopped with knives—metal can taint and discolour these tender-leaved herbs. Check the salad for seasoning and to see that it has enough dressing to moisten it nicely, then serve straight away.
SERVES 6–7

CUCUMBER MOUSSE WITH HERBS AND PRAWNS

This is my mother's recipe and my number one choice for lunch in the garden as it is so deliciously English. It is also agreeably quick and easy to prepare. The herbs can be tossed with the prawns or mixed into the cucumber cream, as you wish.

1 large cucumber
caster (superfine) sugar and tarragon vinegar
gelatine powder
¼ pint/⅔ cup (150 ml) good stock
6 oz (175 g) soft cheese
fresh chives and dill
¼ pint/⅔ cup (150 ml) whipping cream
at least ¾ lb (350 g) boiled and shelled prawns (shrimp)

Peel the cucumber, halve it and scoop out the seeds. Dice the flesh and put it into a bowl, adding 1 scant tsp each salt and caster sugar and 1 tbsp tarragon vinegar. Toss lightly, cover and set aside for at least half an hour to draw out some of the cucumber juices.

Sprinkle 1 very slightly heaped tbsp gelatine powder on to 3 tbsp cold water and leave for 5 minutes or so until the gelatine softens and swells, then beat in the hot stock to dissolve the gelatine to a clear liquid. Slowly and carefully beat the gelatine into the soft cheese. Continue beating until the mixture is perfectly smooth and creamy. Set aside until completely cold.

Drain the juices from the cucumber and mix the diced flesh with about 4 tbsp chopped fresh chives, at least the same amount of parsley, and perhaps a little tarragon or chervil or mint or dill. Gently but thoroughly stir the cucumber mixture into the completely cold cheese mixture. Season it generously with salt and pepper and add a tsp or so of sugar and a tbsp or so of vinegar to taste. Aim for a fresh salad flavour, bearing in mind that the addition of the cream will mute flavours a little. Whip the cream to soft peaks and fold it in. Spoon the mixture into a ring mould or kugelhopf which has been rinsed out with cold water. Cover and refrigerate until set.

Unmould the mousse close to serving time and fill the centre with plenty of good fresh prawns, seasoned with a little salt, pepper and perhaps a squeeze of lemon or lime. A plain but perfectly crisp green salad goes very well with this pretty and quintessentially English dish. New potatoes or fresh bread also make good accompaniments.
SERVES 6

COOK'S NOTEBOOK

The only thing you can rely on in an English summer is its unreliability: never bank on the weather being fine, but, like boy scouts, be prepared. Write down now, while you remember them, a list of quick, winning dishes for emergency occasions. Pin the list to your kitchen noticeboard and stock up on the store-cupboard items required. So armed, you should be ready and able to match every change in the weather with a trump card of your own.

There is no need to scrap your original menus completely when the weather turns sour. If, for example, you planned to serve a main-course salad or mousse for lunch in the garden, stick to it—but take the chill off the disappointment of being driven inside by preceding the cold dish with something brilliantly cheering. What could be easier or better than *Bullshot Soup*: good consommé (either canned or home-made) served piping hot with a spirit-raising slug of vodka in it.

For extra panache, accompany the soup with *Caviare Canapés*. These are rounds of French or other bread, quickly brushed with oil and grilled (broiled) until golden, handed round with a bowl of yoghurt or soured cream and a little dish of mock caviare—which you can buy in tins, very reasonably—for everyone to help themselves.

If my proposed lunch menu consisted simply of chilled soup with delicate little sandwiches on the side, I would not abandon the soup, but I would save the sandwiches for teatime and accompany the soup with something more substantial instead if I could, say cheese straws or hot herb bread. And I would certainly follow the soup with something hot. *Cheese Soufflé* would be my first choice. It's so delicious, so cheap, quick and easy—and it never fails to create a little thrill. I love the dramatic moment of hush when it is brought to the table: towering and trembling, crusted with gold, and still creamy in the centre. Only a flaming brandy-soaked Christmas pudding is greeted more rapturously.

Cooks who are nervous of making soufflés may like to serve a soufflé omelette—savoury or sweet—or a dish of pasta or rice. *Spaghetti alla Carbonara*, with its snippets of lightly fried bacon and beaten eggs that scramble when they touch the hot pasta, is a wonderful standby.

Pasta with Walnut Sauce is another winner. To make the sauce, stir roughly chopped and toasted walnuts into well seasoned hot cream—or cream cheese thinned with milk. Even simpler, and more unusual in Britain, is *Pasta all'Aglio*: just toss the cooked pasta in warm virgin olive oil to which a little garlic and a handful of your favourite fresh chopped herbs have been added.

The Italians are a great source of inspiration when you want something simple, speedy and scrumptious. Their rice recipes are particularly versatile, adapting with delicious grace to suit the needs and availabilities of the moment. *Risotto alla Milanese*, for example, traditionally includes bone marrow, saffron or wine. But it will forego these things quite readily and take on beguiling fresh appeal if you use some alternative finishing touch instead. Add a small handful of just about any young vegetable from the garden and the chances are that you will find yourself feasting on an exquisite "new" risotto. My current favourite is *Aromatic Carrot Risotto*, which I garnish with matchstick slivers of baby carrot seasoned with orange zest and chopped mint.

Another fast, soothing and infinitely variable dish is *Hot Potato Salad*. The basis of this very English dish is lots and lots of new potatoes. They must be freshly dug and ideally be no larger than quails' eggs. The smaller the potato the quicker it cooks, and the higher the ratio of skin to flesh the better it tastes and the healthier it is. Steam the potatoes in their skins. Halve or quarter them after cooking (wear oven gloves to protect your hands from scalding), quickly mix them with chopped Spanish onion or spring onions and toss in a very mustardy vinaigrette dressing. Add to the salad bowl either some diced cucumber, or shredded lettuce, mustard and cress, green pepper, sliced olives or any other vegetables that are to hand. Add hot slices of Frankfurter sausages, or snippets of freshly grilled bacon, chunks of canned tuna fish, flakes of smoked mackerel, slivers of cold chicken, duck, gammon or tongue. You could add several of these or none.

The only things to avoid are sad stale leftovers—their rightful destination is the dustbin. Use whatever is fresh and seems complementary. The choice is yours, and half the charm of the dish lies in creating minor variations on a theme each and every time you make it. Experiments of this sort are the way new recipes are born.

AUTUMN

———❧———

Autumn is a blaze of colour and
excitement with a glut of ripening
vegetables, fruits and nuts. My
squirrelling instincts are strong; I
harvest greedily, filling my larder
as full as I can.

Pâtés and Terrines

There was a time when most people associated the word pâté almost exclusively with meat: very rich pâtés stuffed with fatty pork and expensive game, sometimes larded and barded with pork back fat or studded with truffles or pistachio, and sometimes generously sloshed with alcohol as well.

Time and travel have broadened the British imagination—not to mention our tastebuds. The word pâté now embraces a far wider-ranging, and often far lighter-tasting, selection of foods. Pâté includes fish and vegetables as well as meat; it can have a variety of textures and be used for all sorts of serving occasions.

Pâté can be sliceable, spreadable, dippable, and it isn't obligatory to accompany it with butter and toast. Serve it just as it is, or with warm oatcakes on the side; spread it in the hollows of celery sticks; stuff it in pockets of pitta bread; or make a meal of it with baked potatoes and a selection of salads.

Of course the rich meat pâtés of yesteryear still give delicious pleasure: only killjoys rule them out of their lives completely. But a genuine taste for lighter foods is emerging today. Health considerations apart, most people want to eat rich meat pâtés less often, and few now would dream of serving meat pâté as a first course with meat for the main course to follow—a menu pattern which was commonplace just 15 years ago.

Meat pâtés which are delicately freshened by the inclusion of a vegetable are becoming increasingly popular, and two of my three meat recipes include spinach. Fish pâtés are fast gaining fans of all ages.

Vegetable pâtés are, for many, the newest and most pleasing discovery of all. By vegetable pâtés I do not mean those fancy numbers, multi-striped like deckchairs, sometimes served in restaurants, usually listed on the menu as "vegetable terrines" and given a hefty price-tag to match the posher-sounding name. Those unnaturally orderly rows of rather undercooked vegetables suspended in a pretty insipid jelly may be vogueish but I find them tasteless, even distasteful. As a cook and a consumer, I want to get my teeth into simpler, more wholesome offerings. My idea of a good vegetable pâté is something like guacamole, hummus or aubergine (eggplant) caviare. Good honest dishes like these, the simple country cooking of other nations, have inspired my vegetable pâtés.

VEAL AND HAM PATE

Fresh-tasting and handsome, this is a good choice for a buffet. Topped with a traditional decoration of bay leaves and juniper berries, the pâté slices neatly to reveal a bold band of green spinach and nuggets of rosy gammon embedded in a mixture of other meats. Plenty for 8 or more people, depending on the context in which it is served.

½ lb (225 g) each pie veal and gammon rasher (ham slice)
½ lb (225 g) chicken livers
½ lb (225 g) belly of pork (salt pork), boned and
    de-rinded weight
2 cloves garlic, parsley, marjoram, tarragon, and thyme
2 tbsp sherry
1 lb (450 g) fresh spinach
bay leaves and juniper berries

Dice the raw gammon, sprinkle it with the sherry and set aside.

Chop the other meats and season well: I use 1 tbsp each fresh parsley and marjoram, and 2 tsp each fresh tarragon and thyme (or half quantities if using dried herbs), plus 1 garlic clove crushed with some salt and pepper. Put this mixture of meat and herbs through the medium-fine blade of a mincer or chop it finely in a food processor.

Add to the gammon, stir, cover and leave in a cold larder for 4 hours or more to allow the flavours to blend. Fry a small nugget of the mixture to check seasoning and adjust to individual taste.

Thoroughly wash the spinach. Cook, drain and cool it. Squeeze it to extract as much moisture as possible. Chop it and season it with a clove of garlic crushed with a little salt and plenty of pepper.

Layer the pâté in a loaf tin or other suitable dish of approximately 2¼ pint/5⅔ cup (1 litre) capacity, sandwiching the spinach between two meat layers. Top with bay leaves and juniper berries.

Cover with oiled foil, stand the pâté dish in a roasting pan and pour in enough freshly boiled water to come half way up the sides of the pâté dish. Bake at 325°F (160°C), mark 3 for 1½ hours. Remove the foil and bake for 20 minutes more.

Cool the pâté at room temperature, then tilt and pour off surplus juices. Cover with a double thickness of greaseproof paper and weigh down lightly for several hours or overnight.

ROUGH COUNTRY PATE

You could serve this attractive pâté as a first course. But all meat pâtés—even light ones, like this, made with equal weights of meat and spinach—now seem to me just too substantial for the role of appetiser. These days I reserve meat pâtés for the main course, slicing them thickly and accompanying them with crisp salads and baked potatoes or new potatoes steamed in their skins.

¾ lb (350 g) lean belly of pork (salt pork), boned and de-rinded weight
¼ lb (115 g) pig's liver
1 small lemon
garlic, coriander seeds and thyme
1 lb (450 g) fresh spinach or 9 oz (250 g) frozen whole leaf spinach
6–8 long, thin streaky bacon rashers (slices)

Cube the pork and chop the liver roughly. Mince or process both meats to give a fairly coarse texture. Stir in the finely grated zest of the lemon and 1 tbsp lemon juice. Add 2–3 garlic cloves that have been crushed with 1 tsp salt, and 1 tsp coriander seeds, 1 tsp dried thyme—or almost twice as much fresh lemon thyme—and a good grinding of pepper.

Cover and leave the mixture in a cold place for about 4 hours (or overnight if you prefer) to allow flavours to blend. Then fry a small nugget of the mixture to check seasoning, and adjust to individual taste.

Cook the spinach, drain it and let it become cold. Squeeze it in your hands as tightly as possible to extract as much liquid as you can, then chop the spinach finely and mix it with the pork.

De-rind the bacon, cut each rasher in half and stretch it with the back of a knife.

Lightly oil an oval or oblong dish of about 1½ pint/3¾ cup (850 ml) capacity and line it criss-cross fashion, rather like the stripes on the Union flag, with the halved and stretched rashers of bacon.

Pack the pork and spinach mixture into the dish and fold the ends of the bacon rashers over the top. Cover the dish with oiled foil, stand it in a roasting tin containing enough freshly boiled water to come half-way up the sides of the pâté dish and put the pan in the oven. Bake for approximately 1¼ hours at 325°F (160°C), mark 3.

Let the pâté cook for an hour or so, then tilt the tin and pour off surplus juices—save them to add to your stock pot or soup. Cover the pâté with clean greaseproof paper and weigh it down lightly overnight: this will make the pâté easier to slice for serving.

SERVES 6–8

VINEYARD PATE

Pigeon breast gives this pâté a rich, slightly gamey flavour. Save the meaty pigeon carcasses to make soup. Pheasant or partridge can be used instead of pigeon if you prefer: you will need 8 oz (225 g) raw, skinned and boned meat, preferably breast. Like the other meat pâtés given here, this one is for slicing, not for spreading on bread. A lovely choice for a picnic lunch party.

the breasts of 2 pigeons
½ lb (225 g) chicken livers
¾ lb (350 g) belly of pork (salt pork), boneless weight
brandy
the finely grated zest of an orange
juniper berries and allspice
about 8 large vine leaves

Skin the raw pigeon breasts. Cut the flesh into slivers. Put it into a bowl, add 2 tbsp brandy and the orange zest. Cover and set aside. Trim the chicken livers. De-rind the pork. Chop both meats finely in a food processor or pass them through the medium-fine blade of a meat mincer. Season with 3 crushed juniper berries, ½ tsp allspice, 1 heaped tsp salt and a good grinding of pepper. Stir this meaty mixture into the bowl of marinating pigeon breast. Cover and chill for several hours, then fry a small piece to check seasoning and adjust to individual taste.

If using brined vine leaves, soak, rinse and dry them carefully, following instructions on the packet or tin. If using fresh vine leaves, make them pliable by dropping them into a pan of fast-boiling water; cook for 1–1½ minutes, drain well and dry.

Lightly oil a loaf-tin or other dish of approximately 1¼ pint/generous 3 cup (700 ml) capacity. Line it with the leaves, letting the ends hang over the rim of the dish. Pack the pâté mixture into the dish and fold the ends of the leaves over to encase the filling completely. Brush the top of the leaves with a little oil and cover the dish with oiled foil.

Stand the pâté dish in a roasting pan containing enough freshly boiled water to come halfway up the sides of the dish. Bake at 325°F (160°C), mark 3 for 1¾ hours.

Cool the pâté, then tilt and pour off the juices. Cover the pâté, weigh it down lightly and chill overnight.

SERVES 8

LEFT TO RIGHT: VINEYARD PATE (PAGE 75), VEAL AND HAM PATE (PAGE 74), ROUGH COUNTRY PATE (PAGE 75)

BLACK OLIVE PATE

This deliciously pungent and aromatic pâté is good to eat in any weather. I associate it with warm summer evenings in the garden and with long winter evenings when we gather around a roaring log fire. It is just the thing to spread on bread to nibble as you sit with friends, sharing a bottle of wine, chatting the evening away.

9 oz (250 g) black (ripe) olives
oil
1 very small onion
1 garlic clove
½ tsp dried thyme
2 oz/½ stick (50 g) butter

It is absolutely essential to use very olivey fruit for this simple recipe. Unless you are lucky enough to find olives sold in olive oil, you must steep and sweeten them yourself.

Thoroughly rinse olives sold loose, or drain and wash olives sold packed in brine. Dry them carefully and put them into a jar. Pour on some oil—inexpensive olive oil or even sunflower oil if you prefer—enough to cover the olives. Top the jars with screw-top lids and store in a cool larder. It will take two months for the olives to become olivey sweet but if you keep them stored in the oil for longer they will taste even better. Olives prepared this way are best for all cooking and eating purposes, not just for this recipe, and the improvement is so marked that I now automatically treat olives this way every time I buy them. The oil can be re-used many times over.

To make the pâté, drain the required quantity of olives and stone them. Cut the onion into quarters and chop the garlic finely. Put the onion into a food processor or blender and whizz until chopped very finely. Add the prepared olives, garlic and thyme and process again. Then add the butter, which should be at room temperature and cut into dice; add it gradually while the machine is running. When the mixture is reduced to a smooth creamy paste, taste it and add a little salt or more thyme or garlic if you wish.

Press the pâté into a pot, cover and chill it for 24 hours or more before serving to allow flavours to blend and develop. This pâté is particularly good spread on thin rounds of lightly toasted French bread.

SERVES 6–8

LENTIL AND ANCHOVY PATE

This is a little like the famous chick-pea pâté called hummus. Make it with whole lentils, preferably the lovely grey-green lentils from Le Puy, not ordinary split red lentils. Anchovy fillets give the pulses an appealing smoky flavour and lemon juice adds agreeable sharpness. Serve this soft-textured pâté alone or, better still, in company with one or more other vegetable pâtés. It is suitable for spreading or dipping and makes a good first course for lunch or dinner. It is delicious served with a selection of raw vegetables for dipping: strips of green pepper, sticks of cucumber (seeded but unpeeled), sprigs of cauliflower, baby radishes, finger carrots and so on. Lentil and Anchovy Pâté keeps well for several days and is so useful that I often make a double quantity while I am at it.

3 oz/scant ½ cup (75 g) whole green lentils
olive oil
1½ oz/3 tbsp (40 g) chopped onion
juice of half a large lemon
2 oz (50 g) can of anchovy fillets

Thoroughly rinse the lentils—there is no need to soak them. Pick them over carefully and drain well. Warm 1 tbsp olive oil in a heavy-based pan. Add the lentils and onion and stir over a low heat for a few minutes to coat entirely with fat.

Add the juice of half a large lemon and 12 fl oz/ 1½ cups (350 ml) warm water. Cover the pan and leave to simmer gently for 1 hour.

Add the canned anchovies (cut into snippets) and their oil. Cover the pan again and simmer for 15 minutes more or until the lentils are perfectly tender.

Drain off any liquid remaining in the pan and reserve it. Let the solids cool slightly, then tip them into a food processor or blender and reduce to a thick purée. Then beat in 1 tbsp or so each of the cooking liquid and olive oil to give the mixture a creamy consistency suitable for spreading (or thin with a good quantity of each if you want to use the mixture as a dip) and add extra seasoning to taste. Cool, pack into a small dish, cover and chill.

SERVES 6–8

COOK'S NOTEBOOK

It was once commonplace to see shoppers glide down supermarket aisles, as blind and as sure-footed as sleepwalkers, transferring items from shelf to trolley with barely a glance at what they were buying. No longer. A few people still shop like that, but not many. Supermarkets are increasingly assuming the quiet and studious air of libraries: just as the would-be borrower of a book scans the dust-jacket blurb, flicks through several chapters and reads a few sample paragraphs before deciding whether to borrow, so the food shopper is beginning to scrutinise the goods on offer more thoroughly before deciding whether to buy.

Most of us are prepared to pay a reasonable price for a reasonable product, and we don't mind too much being asked to pay a premium for something that makes genuinely superior eating. What we do object to is being asked to pay through the nose for a product that is not good to eat or that turns out to be little more than pretty packaging, or both.

Marketing people know full well that the new-found interest in a healthier way of eating has increased the lure of country things. All that chintzy watercolour packaging is meant to imply "country", "traditional" and "wholesome", and words like these are much used and abused on labels for products that may be, in fact, little more than chemical cocktails dreamt up in some city factory.

We need a guide to advertising-speak and label-language to distinguish between honest truth and manipulated facts.

There is one sure way to avoid falling prey to the ploys of cunning marketing. Shut your eyes resolutely to pretty packaging and flowery verbiage, turn straight to the small discreet panel on the back of the pack: the ingredients list, where the truth is harder to hide. Mind you, strictly factual though the ingredients list may be, reading it can be quite hard work. We know that ingredients are listed in order of proportion used, beginning with the major item. We know too, that E numbers represent EEC permitted additives: colourants, preservatives, antioxidants, emulsifiers and stabilisers. But you really need a degree in chemistry and a truly marvellous memory to decipher it all—the average ingredients label contains hardly any plain English words.

The following ingredients list is quite brief and straightforward compared with many: "salt, beef fat (with antioxidant E320), monosodium glutamate, yeast extract, dehydrated cod, chicken fat (with antioxidant E320), onion powder, flavouring, spices and herbs."

I dare say you will share my view that, sadly, it does not read, and certainly does not taste, like the product it purports to be—fish stock cubes.

The use of some additives is almost inevitable in processed or "recipe" foods. Every cook adds things while cooking. Most of us add a little salt to pasta, rice or vegetables. We may use a little cornflour to stabilise an egg custard.

It may be undesirable but it is surely understandable that manufacturers use more stabilisers, emulsifiers, antioxidants and other preservatives than we do:

our home cooking is usually for immediate eating, their products aim for longer safe keeping.

Having said that, I regard the use of some additives as very questionable, if not downright objectionable. The yellow azo-dye tartrazine (E102) is a case in point. Like all colourants it is purely cosmetic, so it is unnecessary and seems possibly harmful to some, in particular to certain children. It is widely used in smoked haddock and also smoked cod.

There has been a lot of publicity about how parents of hyperactive children have found remarkable benefit in putting their children on tartrazine-free diets. As a result of all this new consumer awareness, some manufacturers (only some) have started to remove tartrazine and other contentious chemical dyes from their products.

This is a great step forward. But remember: the proud boast "free from artificial colourants" plastered across the front of a pack does not mean free from added colour. In most cases, products that were coloured with artificial dyes such as tartrazine are now being coloured with vegetable dyes such as crocin instead. These "natural" vegetable dyes may not be branded as "possibly harmful", but why should the use of any added colour be considered desirable?

Some stores are now offering undyed smoked haddock: fish of a pale and creamy hue which is naturally acquired during smoking. I shall ask for it locally and I'll travel further afield to buy it if necessary. I hope you will too. For asking often and loudly enough is the only way to get what we want in our shops.

SMOKED SALMON DÉLICE

SMOKED SALMON DELICE

These individual-size pâtés look as splendid as they taste, but, somewhat surprisingly perhaps, they are child's play to make. I rate them as an excellent choice for a dinner party when you want to serve a simple but stunning first course. The better the smoked salmon the better the pâté of course—be sure to have it sliced very thinly for this dish.

about 7 oz (200 g) smoked salmon
generous 10 oz (300 g) white fish fillets, such as haddock
    or whiting
lemon juice and olive oil
fresh parsley and chives or dill
4 oz (125 g) soft cheese, such as Philadelphia or St Moret

Skin and bone the white fish and cut the flesh into tiny pieces. Sprinkle it with the juice of a large lemon and set aside in a cool place for 2–3 hours until the fish is "cooked" and translucent.

Lightly oil 6–8 cocotte dishes of 3 fl oz/generous ⅓ cup (75 ml) capacity and lay sprigs of flat-leafed parsley or dill on the base of each. Then line the dishes with the smoked salmon, letting a little surplus hang over the rims. Drain the white fish well, reserving the marinating juices, and put it into a food processor. Add 1 generous tbsp olive oil and any leftover smoked salmon and process to a smooth purée. Add the soft cheese, 1 tbsp chopped parsley and a *soupçon* of chopped chives or dill and process again. Season the mixture to taste and sharpen it with a drop of the reserved marinating juices or enrich it with a little more oil if you think it necessary. A lot depends on the smoked salmon used.

Divide the fish purée between the dishes, press it down firmly with a teaspoon and fold the ends of the smoked salmon over to encase the filling completely. Cover and refrigerate for 4 hours or more to allow flavours to blend.

Unmould the fishy parcels on to individual plates to serve. (They should slip out of the dishes quite readily: bring them to room temperature a few minutes before unmoulding and run a knife around the edge of each dish immediately before inverting it on to a plate.)

Decorate each plate with a few salad leaves if you wish. Oatcakes or water biscuits which have been gently warmed in a low oven go well with this pâté, which should be eaten with a knife and fork.

SERVES 6–8

CREAMY CARROT PATE

The ingredients list for this recipe looks very unpromising but the resulting pâté makes excellent eating. The character of the dish is radically changed by the inclusion or omission of the curry powder, but both versions seem equally popular. It's a good pâté for spreading on warm pitta bread, oatcakes or water biscuits to nibble with pre-prandial drinks. Sometimes I serve it alone, but I like even better to serve it with a couple of other pâtés alongside it: Courgette Pâté with Green Herbs and Rich Mushroom Pâté make good partners for it.

½ lb (225 g) carrots
1½ tbsp olive oil
1 small orange
1 small onion
sugar
pinch of curry powder (optional)
1 tsp wholegrain mustard
2 tbsp mayonnaise (home-made or shop-bought)

Slice the carrots and chop the onion finely. Warm the olive oil in a saucepan. Stir in the onion, cover and leave to sweat gently for 7–8 minutes.

Add the carrots, the juice and finely grated zest of the orange, 1 scant tsp sugar and a good grinding of pepper. Add the curry powder if you wish to include it. Stir to mix well and add just enough water to cover the carrots. Cover the pan tightly and leave to simmer gently until the vegetables are perfectly tender. They will probably take rather longer than usual to cook—the citrus juice seems to slow down the tenderising process.

When the carrots are ready, remove the lid and continue cooking, stirring as necessary, until the liquid has evaporated. Set the pan aside, uncovered, until the contents are quite cool.

Empty the contents of the pan into a food processor or blender and reduce to a purée. Stop the machine and push the vegetables down on to the blades as often as is necessary to achieve perfectly smooth results. Add 1 tsp mustard, 2 tbsp mayonnaise and a pinch of salt and process again.

Check and adjust seasoning to taste before pressing the pâté into a small dish. Level the top, cover and refrigerate for several hours before serving.

SERVES 6–8

COURGETTE PATE WITH GREEN HERBS

This is an exceptionally light pâté: fairly soft in texture, a pretty pale green and fragrantly scented with fresh green herbs. A very useful recipe for using up courgettes that have grown a bit too big to make a delicate cooked vegetable. Spread the pâté on bread or biscuits or slacken the mixture slightly and use it as a cool dip for raw vegetables.

½ lb (225 g) courgettes (zucchini)
tarragon vinegar or white wine vinegar
caster (superfine) sugar
a large bunch of fresh parsley
a large bunch of fresh chives
3 oz (75 g) Philadelphia or cream cheese

Top and tail the courgettes but do not peel them. Grate them coarsely and put them into a bowl. Sprinkle on 1 tsp tarragon or wine vinegar, and 1 tsp sugar plus ½ tsp salt. Toss gently, cover and set aside for 45 minutes (or for several hours if more convenient) to draw out some of the courgettes' moisture.

Chop a good quantity of fresh parsley, enough to come up to the 5 fl oz/⅔ cup (150 ml) level when packed fairly tightly in a measuring jug. Then snip a similar quantity of chives. Put both herbs into a food processor or blender and push them well down on to the blades. Stopping and starting the machine as necessary, reduce the herbs to fine green flecks.

Drain the courgettes in a sieve then squeeze them with your hands to extract as much liquid as possible. Add the compressed gratings to the machine and process again. Then add the soft cheese in little nuggets, and process once more to blend ingredients thoroughly. Season to taste with salt and pepper and pack the pâté into a small dish. Cover and chill for 1 hour or more before serving.

The best breads to serve with these fresh green flavours are granary bread, fingers of warm pitta bread, rye bread or good brown bread.

SERVES 6–8

COUNTRY POTTED PRAWNS

White fish fillets and prawns are used in equal quantities in this traditional fish pâté, which has an excellent shellfish flavour. It is the sort of dish that used to take pride of place on the table at Sunday high tea. Today we are more likely to serve it with fingers of brown toast for a first course at dinner, or with wedges of warm soda bread and a large fresh salad as a light lunch dish for 6–8 people.

¾ lb (350 g) cooked prawns (shrimp) in their shells
¾ lb (350 g) fresh haddock, cod or coley fillets
coriander seeds and fresh or dried basil
anchovy essence (extract) and sweet paprika
¼ lb/1 stick (115 g) each salted and clarified butter

Shell the prawns. Put the shells into a pan with water to cover, plus some crushed coriander seeds and basil. Bring to the boil, cover and simmer gently for 25 minutes.

Process briefly to crush and chop the shells, then strain every drop of the shellfish-flavoured liquid through a fine sieve.

Season the prawn stock generously with salt and pepper, and poach the fish fillets in it: 10–15 minutes is enough to cook them nicely. Strain the prawn stock again afterwards and save it for using in other dishes—refrigerate it if you plan to use it within 1–2 days; freeze it for longer storage.

Skin, bone and flake the fish fillets. Chop them very finely in a food processor. Add a good shake of anchovy essence, about ⅛ tsp paprika and the salted butter (at room temperature and cut into small dice). Process again to make a perfectly smooth and well blended purée.

Barely melt the clarified butter. Beat most of it into the fish purée, adding it gradually while the food processor is running. Take the buttery fish purée out of the machine and gently but thoroughly mix it with the prawns (which should be roughly chopped with a sharp knife). Check and adjust seasoning to taste: the mixture should be agreeably fishy and spicy and slightly pink in colour. Texture should be good and thick: if it seems very stiff, beat in a teaspoon or two of the shellfish stock.

Pack the delicious fishy mixture into a pot, pressing it down firmly, and pour on the rest of the melted butter to seal. As soon as the contents are completely cold, cover the pot with cling film and chill until shortly before serving.

RICH MUSHROOM PATE

I always think that mushrooms, like aubergines, deserve to be described as "poor man's meat", for compared with green vegetables, they are so rich-tasting and filling. They make a glorious and intriguingly flavoured pâté which is one of my favourites to serve with pre-dinner drinks. It is of course cheapest and best when made with mushrooms you have picked yourself.

generous ½ lb (250 g) dark field mushrooms or large flat
   mushrooms
1 small onion
cumin and coriander seeds
2 oz/½ stick (50 g) each salted and unsalted butter
1 tbsp Marsala
a shake each of soy and Worcestershire sauce
1 tsp mushroom ketchup

Wipe the mushrooms and discard the stalks. Slice the mushrooms fairly thickly, then cut across into cubes. Chop the onion quite finely.

Warm 1 tsp each cumin and coriander seeds in a frying pan over medium-low heat until toasty and warm and aromatic. Pound the spices to a powder with mortar and pestle.

Put the unsalted butter into the frying pan. When melted add the onion and cook very gently for about 10 minutes until thoroughly softened. Remove with a slotted spoon. Add the mushrooms to the pan. Increase heat to medium-high and fry for 6 minutes or so, stirring and turning the mushrooms until they are reduced in bulk and most of their moisture has been driven off. Add the Marsala to the pan and switch off the heat. Return the onions to the pan. Add the prepared spices, soy sauce, Worcestershire sauce and 1 tsp mushroom ketchup. Stir to mix everything well then aside until cool but not cold.

Empty the contents of the pan into a food processor or blender and reduce to a fine black-flecked purée. Push the mixture well down on to the blades and stop and start the machine often for smooth results. Add the salted butter which should be at room temperature and cut into small dice, and process again to make a smooth cream. Season to taste.

Spoon the pâté into a small dish which has been lightly brushed with oil. Push it down into the corners and level the top. Cover and chill for several hours before serving but bring the pâté back to room temperature about 1 hour before serving to soften it slightly. Fingers of warm pitta bread or granary bread make admirable accompaniments.
SERVES 6–8

SMOKED MACKEREL PATE WITH GOOSEBERRY

Smoked mackerel pâté can be very smooth and sometimes seems to contain more cream or butter than fish. This version has an interesting texture and a rich fishy flavour, which is nicely tempered by a sharp gooseberry sauce. Use whole mackerel rather than mackerel which has been filleted before smoking. The flesh of the latter often has a tough surface "skin" and it lacks the true mackerel taste of fish smoked on the bone.

2 plump smoked mackerel, weighing 1¼–1½ lb
   (600–700 g) in total
lemon juice, French and wholegrain mustard
2 tbsp each soured cream and mayonnaise
scant 1 lb (400 g) cooking gooseberries

Fillet the mackerel, skin and bone it. There should be about 14 oz/2⅓ cups (400 g) usuable fish. Flake it into a large soup plate or shallow bowl.

Add a squeeze of lemon and a good grinding of pepper and crush lightly with a fork. Stir ½ tsp of both mustards, the soured cream and mayonnaise together until smoothly mixed. Add the mixture to the fish, a little at a time, working it in gently with a fork.

The flavourings must be well blended with the fish of course, but the pâté will be better to look at and to eat if it is slightly knobbly in texture, like good tweed, not reduced to babyfood pappiness. Taste and add extra mustard, pepper, lemon and/or salt as you wish. If the consistency seems too stiff, work in a little more soured cream or mayonnaise, but take care not to make the mixture sloppy or to dilute the fishy flavour too much. Consistency should be firm but spreadable; taste should be distinctly mackerel and well seasoned.

Turn the pâté into a pot or pots, cover and chill.

Put the gooseberries into a saucepan—no need to top or tail them—together with 1–2 tbsp water. Cover and simmer gently, shaking the pan occasionally until the fruit is quite soft. Crush the berries with a potato masher, increase heat a little and cook, stirring almost continuously, until most of the liquid is driven off. Rub the fruit through a sieve and let it become cold. Sweeten the purée with a little icing (confectioners') sugar if you wish, but keep it sharp to foil the richness of the pâté.

Top the pâté with the cold sauce immediately before serving and serve with plenty of hot wholemeal toast. No need to use butter.
SERVES 8 OR MORE

Cooking with Cider

Cider has been the countryman's drink for centuries, and cider-making used to be a major social event. On late autumn evenings, anyone who had apples might take the fruit to a neighbouring farm which had a cider press. Others from surrounding hamlets would gather there, bringing with them apples with glorious names such as Warrenden, Foxwhelp, Longstreak Redstreak, Slack My Girdle, Bloody Butcher, Kingston Black and Handsome Maud. Everyone would share in the communal tasks of washing the fruit and crushing it to a pulp in stone or wooden presses till the juices ran freely. By the early hours of the morning the assembled company would be tired and possibly quite merry. During the course of the night's work, they might well have helped to drink the last of the previous season's vintage—and farmhouse cider, or scrumpy or tanglefoot as it is variously called, can be potent stuff, quite capable of reducing strong men to a state resembling drowsy bumble-bees.

Although most cider today is produced commercially, some is still made privately, in small traditional presses on farms and in cottages in apple-growing areas. There is no reason why you should not—like Joe Grundy of *The Archers*—make your own home-brew. And there is every reason why you should consider using cider in cooking as well as for drinking. Cider can be used in the kitchen to delicious advantage in all sorts of ways: it's more than just an alternative to wine, for cider has the twin virtues of tasting fresh and fruity and, what's more, it's cheaper.

It is the natural choice of liquid to use when cooking orchard fruits such as apples, pears and plums, and hedgerow fruits such as blackberries. It is excellent as the liquid in a batter for pancakes to be filled with apples or other fruits; it is perfect for plumping dried fruits to be used in tea-breads and cakes; and lovely for braising autumn vegetables such as leeks and red cabbage.

Cider goes well with cheese and makes a fine partner for shellfish. Because it is light, fruity and elegant, it does not overpower delicate white meats such as rabbit, veal, chicken, brains and sweet-breads. Moreover, because cider is acidic it cuts down the richness of fatty foods. Oily fish like mackerel and herring benefit from being dressed with cider and apples, as do rich meats like pork, gammon, duck and goose, and meats with a very pronounced flavour, like oxtail.

Cider can be used raw for mild appley aroma. It can be mixed with oil and herbs to make marinades, when it will add subtle flavour and help to break down tough fibres. Or the amber liquid can be heated, in which case the alcohol evaporates, the liquid reduces and the flavour becomes more concentrated and mellow. This reduction occurs naturally in a long, slow cooking process, such as casseroling, when the flavours of all the ingredients in the pot are deliciously blended as the food becomes tender. Or it can be achieved quickly by fast boiling the cider over high heat until reduced by about half.

If, on special occasions, you want to give a dish a little more oomph than cider alone will provide, you might like to use a mixture of cider reduced by fast boiling and a little whisky. This combination is a British approximation of the well known French apple-jack brandy called Calvados, and I have used it in the recipe for Tanglefoot Rabbit, right.

If, on the other hand, you prefer fresher, more fruity-tasting foods, or you want to avoid alcohol, use unsweetened apple juice instead of cider to flavour recipes. For an even sharper edge, add a dash of cider vinegar. This can also be used as a substitute for cider or apple juice on occasions when you have neither in the house: simply crush a sugar cube in a tablespoon or so of cider vinegar, dilute with cold water and add a little extra sugar if it is appropriate for the recipe.

Cider vinegar, incidentally, is quite easy to make at home. You need still dry (hard) cider to make it—not sweet or fizzy cider—and just a spoonful of vinegar (cider vinegar, wine vinegar or malt vinegar) to act as the "starter". Half-fill a scrupulously clean plastic bucket with still dry cider. Add 1 tbsp vinegar and beat with a balloon whisk for 2 minutes to aerate the mixture well.

Cover the bucket with a piece of buttermuslin or some other open-weave cloth and leave undisturbed in a corner of the kitchen or some other warm room until the liquid has turned to vinegar. It will probably take no more than six or seven days to turn: you will know when it is ready by the characteristic vinegary smell. Bottle, label and store the vinegar in a cool larder, where it will keep well for at least two years.

TANGLEFOOT RABBIT

Tanglefoot is an old West Country name for strong farmhouse cider—very descriptive of the effect of the liquor on the drinker. In this recipe cider is combined with spirits and a good deal of cream to make an exceedingly rich and subtle-tasting sauce for a dish of rabbit and fresh field mushrooms. Wild rabbit is traditional, of course, but farmed rabbit is just as suitable and some supermarkets now sell packs of excellent quality selected joints of fresh farmed English rabbit. Leg fillets or shoulder joints are especially good for this dish.

1 rabbit, jointed, or about 2–2½ lb (1 kg) selected rabbit joints
¾ lb/6 cups (350 g) mushrooms
12 fl oz/1½ cups (350 ml) still dry cider
3–4 tbsp whisky
½ pint/1¼ cups (275 ml) double (heavy) cream
1 oz/¼ stick (30 g) clarified or unsalted butter
coriander seeds and fresh parsley

Dust the rabbit with plenty of crushed coriander seeds and pepper and a little salt. Seal and colour the meat, in batches, in ½ oz/1 tbsp (15 g) butter in a very hot frying pan. Transfer the browned rabbit to a flameproof casserole in which you have heated the cider.

Set the frying pan aside: do not wash it up as the buttery rabbit sediment it contains will be needed later. Cover the casserole and cook at 300°F (150°C), mark 2 until the rabbit is perfectly tender; 1½ hours is about right for hutch rabbit, wild rabbit may need 2–2½ hours.

Transfer the cooked rabbit to a warmed serving platter, cover and keep hot. Reduce the cidery cooking liquid to 4 fl oz/½ cup (100 ml) or just under by fast boiling.

While the liquid is reducing, sauté the thickly sliced mushrooms in the frying pan using ½ oz/1 tbsp (15 g) butter. Arrange the mushrooms over the rabbit and season them with salt, pepper and coriander.

Pour the reduced cider into the frying pan, add the whisky and flambé. When the flames have died down, pour on the cream. Return the pan to the heat and cook, stirring continuously, until the ingredients are smoothly blended and the sauce is bubbling hot and slightly thickened—about 5 minutes.

Season the sauce to taste, pour it over the rabbit, cover again and return to the oven for at least 15 minutes before serving. This rich dish is best garnished with plenty of fresh chopped parsley and accompanied by plain boiled rice. Serve vegetables as a separate course.
SERVES 5–6

PIPPIN FLAN WITH CIDER CREAM SAUCE

Elegant and pretty, yet easy to make, this is my favourite fruit flan. Ideally it should be made on the day of serving: it is best warm, rather than piping hot, but it is also very good cold. I specify using Cox's Orange Pippins because they are far and away the best—crisp and sweet with a hint of sharpness. Bland apples are just as bad in cooking as they are to eat raw.

1 × 10 inch (25 cm) shortcrust pastry flan case, thoroughly blind baked
2¼ lb (1 kg) Cox's apples
a little unsalted butter and honey
¼ pint/⅔ cup (150 ml) medium-sweet cider
2 tbsp semolina or ground almonds
½ pint/1¼ cups (275 ml) thick creamy yoghurt, Greek or home-made

Peel, core and quarter the apples, reserving the peels and cores. Slice them, but not too thinly. Fry them in a little butter over medium-low heat for about 5 minutes so the apples become slightly softened, translucent and streaked with pale gold. If you use a 12 inch (30 cm) frying pan you should be able to cook the apples in two batches. Do not use more than 2 oz/½ stick (50 g) butter in all or the apple will taste greasy and be too slippery to handle.

Sprinkle the semolina or ground almonds over the pastry base to stop moisture seeping into it during cooking, then arrange the slightly cooled apple slices in the flan prettily in circles, standing them almost upright and packing them quite closely—as shown in the photograph, page 89.

Bake the flan at 400°F (200°C), mark 6 for about 30 minutes.

Meanwhile, simmer the apple peel and cores with the cider in a covered pan for about 20 minutes, stirring occasionally, until everything is tender. Strain through a sieve, pressing the softened pulp gently to extract all the juices. There should be 2 fl oz/¼ cup (60 ml)—boil down to reduce, or dilute what there is with water, if necessary. Stir in 2–3 tsp honey. Beat *half* this mixture into the yoghurt and chill it to serve instead of pouring cream with the flan.

Beat 2 or more tbsp honey into the remaining mixture to make a sweet thick glaze. Brush the glaze over the cooked apple flan and slide the flan under the grill (broiler) briefly to give it a golden-topped finish.
SERVES 8

ORCHARD TOASTED CHEESE

Some rarebits and other toasted cheese recipes are almost too rich and cheesy for my taste. This version is lighter than most. It makes a lovely quick lunch dish: a useful hot alternative to the so-called ploughman's platter of bread, pickle and cheese. And it is pretty enough to serve at a party. Only a splash of cider is used in the recipe but if the dish is made in the old-fashioned West Country manner the ham might well come from a pig which has roamed the orchards and fed on windfall cider apples; and I recommend cider to accompany the eating of Orchard Toasted Cheese. The success of this exceedingly simple dish depends almost entirely on using top-quality ingredients: really good ham, farmhouse cheeses and fine fruit—English Cox's, not the dreaded Golden Delicious from France. Serves four as a lunch dish or eight as a snack.

3 each large ripe dessert apples and pears
a large bunch of grapes
8 small thin slices of crusty bloomer loaf
cider, lemon and mild mustard
4 large slices of ham, freshly carved from the bone
4–5 oz/1–1¼ cups (115–150 g) each Lancashire and
    Farmhouse Cheddar cheese, grated and mixed

Quarter the apples and pears and remove cores. Don't peel the fruit but cut the quarters into thick slices. Dip the slices as soon as prepared in a mixture of lemon juice and cider (the juice of half a lemon plus 4 tbsp cider) to prevent discolouration. Shake off excess liquid, arrange the fruit decoratively on plates and garnish prettily with the grapes, broken into very small bunches.

Toast the bread well on one side and lightly on the other. Splash the lightly toasted side with a little cider—only a tsp or so will be needed per slice. Spread each slice with a little mustard, cover with a half slice of ham and sprinkle some cheese over the top.

Lay the toasts side by side on a baking tray and slide them under a medium-hot grill (broiler)—avoid fierce heat as it spoils the cheese, making it stringy and tough. Cook until the cheese is melted and hot and is freckled here and there with delicate golden-brown blisters.

Transfer the toasts to the plates and serve straight away. The idea is to nibble the fruit between mouthfuls of the hot toast, the clean tastes of the fruit providing a lovely foil for the richness of the ham and the cheese.

CIDER-SOUSED MACKEREL

Mackerel prepared this way will keep for a week providing they remain immersed in the liquid. Herring is a good alternative to mackerel. Serve the fish as an appetiser for eight as described here, or as a lunch dish for four. At lunchtime I accompany the fish with a green salad: crisp lettuce and watercress, generously scattered with apple slices and crescent-moon slivers of celery.

4 mackerel, filleted
1 onion
4 cloves
3 bay leaves
6 peppercorns
¼ pint/⅔ cup (150 ml) or more cider vinegar—see method
¾ pint/scant 2 cups (450 ml) or more dry cider—see method

Put the fish fillets into a deep flameproof dish. Peel the onion and cut it into wafer-thin slices. Bruise the cloves lightly with mortar and pestle, or give them a gentle bash with the end of a rolling-pin. Bruise half a dozen peppercorns in the same way.

Scatter the onion and bay leaves over the fish, sprinkle on the bruised spices and pour on first the vinegar and then the cider. The fish should be completely immersed in the liquid: if necessary add more, using the ratio given—that is three parts cider to one part vinegar.

Place the dish over the lowest possible heat and bring it very slowly indeed to the boil. Leave it to bubble for 1 minute, then draw the dish away from the heat and allow the contents to become completely cold. Cover the dish tightly and refrigerate until needed.

To serve, carefully lift out of the dish as many fish fillets as are required, using a fish slice and slotted spoon to lift them. Lay the fillets on a platter and drizzle just a spoonful or so of the pickling liquor over them.

Decorate with a bay leaf or two or garnish with a clump of watercress and some slices of unpeeled dessert apple. The apple slices should be dipped in the pickling liquor to keep them fresh-looking.

Accompany the mackerel with good wholemeal bread and unsalted butter, or with unbuttered rye bread and hand round a large bowl of creamy yoghurt.

OXTAIL WITH APPLE

Less robust than most oxtail casseroles, this one is deliciously fruity: it contains apples and cider and has a faint background hint of curry spices. I find it just right for serving on cool autumn evenings—and it is worth making a good quantity as it freezes very well indeed.

4 lb (1.8 kg) oxtail, cut into 2 inch (5 cm) pieces
1 lb (450 g) dessert apples
2 onions
sunflower oil
¾ pint/scant 2 cups (425 ml) dry cider
½ pint/1¼ cups (275 ml) beef stock
mild curry powder or paste and a bay leaf
a little butter and flour

Begin cooking the day before you want to serve the casserole. Trim as much fat as possible from the oxtail. Colour the meat all over in a large, shallow flameproof casserole that has been barely filmed with oil.

Remove the meat and colour the very finely chopped onions. Stir in ¾–1 tsp mild curry powder or paste and 1 generous tsp of flour. Pour on the dry cider and beef stock and bring to the boil, stirring.

Return the meat to the casserole and cook at a fast simmer for about 10 minutes without a lid, until the liquid is somewhat reduced.

Add a large bay leaf, plenty of salt and pepper, cover the casserole and cook in the oven at 275–300°F (140–150°C), mark 1–2 for 1½ hours.

Turn the pieces of meat over, cover again and continue cooking in the oven for a further hour or until the meat is tender and beginning to come away from the bones.

Cool and chill the casserole overnight, then scrape away and discard the layer of fat that will have solidified on the surface of the liquid. Peel and core the apples and cut them into thick slices, fry them in batches in as little butter as possible until slightly softened and attractively gilded.

Meanwhile, reheat the casserole gently but very thoroughly indeed. Check the gravy for seasoning and simmer without a lid until the gravy is reduced to a good consistency. Gently stir in the apples immediately before serving. A crisp watercress salad and lots of creamy mashed potatoes go well with this dish.

SERVES 6–7

PIPPIN FLAN WITH CIDER CREAM SAUCE (PAGE 85)

Herb-Garden Jelly

Cider vinegar gives this savoury jelly an agreeable tang. The use of a mixture of fresh herbs means that the jelly goes well with a variety of meats, poultry and fish, but you could use just one sort of herb if you prefer. Fragrant home-made jellies are lovely to have in the store cupboard for winter eating and they make very attractive Christmas presents.

4 lb (1.8 kg) Bramleys
fresh parsley and mint (preferably apple mint)
fresh thyme (preferably lemon thyme) and tarragon
½ pint/1¼ cups (250 ml) cider vinegar
granulated sugar

Wash the apples and quarter them, discarding any damaged parts; there is no need to peel or core them. Put them into a food processor in batches, together with a dozen or so parsley stalks and 4 or 5 sprigs each of mint, thyme and tarragon, and process until chopped to small pieces. Chopping the fruit like this helps to speed up the release of the pectin and makes for a fairly quick cooking time.

Tip the chopped fruit and herbs into a large pan. Add 2 pints/5 cups (1.1 litres) cold water. Do not add the water directly to the saucepan but add it via the bowl of the food processor: this way you will "rinse out" and add to the saucepan any apple juice and small pieces of fruit that may remain in the processing bowl.

Simmer gently until the fruit is reduced to a meltingly tender mush—I allow 25 minutes. Stir in the vinegar and bring quickly to a fast boil, then tip the contents of the pan into a scalded jelly bag suspended over a deep bowl and leave until the liquid has dripped through.

Measure the lightly herb-flavoured juices, put them into a preserving pan and add 1 lb/scant 2¼ cups (450 g) sugar for every 1 pint/2½ cups (600 ml) liquid. Clip a thermometer to the side of the pan and stir over low heat until the sugar has dissolved.

Bring to the boil and boil rapidly until setting point is reached, that is when the temperature reads 220°F (104°C). Check setting point by using the traditional saucer test as well.

Away from the heat, stir in some chopped fresh herbs; for 12 small jars of well flavoured and well flecked jelly I use about 8 tbsp fresh chopped parsley, 6 of mint and just 1 each of thyme and tarragon.

Let the mixture stand for about 10 minutes so it cools slightly and starts setting. Then stir gently to ensure the herbs are evenly distributed and will remain suspended in the jelly. Pot into warm clean jars.

ENOUGH FOR 12 SMALL JARS

Apple Fritters with Syllabub Sauce

Quite simply, this scrumptious pudding is a very greedy treat. Save it for a rainy day when you plan to forget all about calories and cholesterol.

6 dessert apples
ground cinnamon and allspice
a little lemon juice and icing (confectioners') sugar
about 7 fl oz/scant 1 cup (200 ml) unsweetened apple
   juice or still dry cider
¼ pint/⅔ cup (150 ml) double (heavy) cream
4 oz/scant 1 cup (100 g) plain (all-purpose) flour
2 tbsp sunflower or safflower oil
2 egg whites

First make the syllabub sauce, which can be prepared several hours ahead. Put ¼–½ tsp ground cinnamon into a mixing bowl. Add a scant 1 oz/¼ cup (25 g) icing sugar, then stir in 1 tbsp lemon juice and 4 tbsp still dry cider or unsweetened apple juice.

Slowly pour on the cream, stirring the contents of the bowl with a balloon whisk all the time as you do so. Continue whisking the mixture until it holds a soft shape. It should not be stiff. Set aside in a cool place until ready to serve.

The first stage in making the batter can also be done well ahead: sift the flour into a bowl together with about ¼ tsp each ground cinnamon and allspice. Make a well in the centre. Put the oil into the well and ¼ pint/⅔ cup (150 ml) still dry cider or unsweetened apple juice. Gradually beat the liquids into the dry ingredients to make a smooth creamy batter. Set aside until ready to cook.

When ready to serve, heat the oil for frying in a deep-fat pan, with a thermometer clipped to the side of the pan. Peel, core and slice the apples into rings. Sprinkle with a little lemon juice. Whisk the egg whites until stiff and fold them into the batter to make it extra light.

Make the fritters in small batches: pat a few apple slices dry to mop up the lemon juice, dip them into the batter and shake off excess. Deep fry at 360°F (185°C) or just over until hot, well cooked and a beautiful golden-brown. Each batch will take 4–5 minutes. Drain well and keep hot in a single layer in the oven until all are ready—do not cover the fritters or they will lose their delicious crispness. Serve piping hot, dusted with a little icing sugar or cinnamon if you like, and hand around the cool creamy syllabub sauce separately.

SERVES 4–6

COOK'S NOTEBOOK

This is the time when everything in the garden seems to indulge in a final flamboyant fling. It's just like standing in the middle of one of those Walt Disney nature films, in which things are speeded up to show the whole life-cycle of a flower in seconds. Cooks are hard put to keep pace with such a flood of fruits, vegetables, fungi and berries—but they keep on trying. There is something hypnotic about it all. Just as it is well nigh impossible to resist dipping one's hand back, time and time again, into a bowl of cherries or a box of chocolates, so cooks feel impelled to carry on picking, cooking and bottling in an autumn glut.

However rotten the summer weather, or poor the gardener, there's no stopping courgettes (zucchini). Like triffids, they seem to multiply and to take a step closer every time you turn around. Make them into soups, pâtés and fritters; steam, stir-fry, stuff and bake them and there are always more awaiting your attention. I use a lot to make a *Courgette Salad* which keeps well for several days. Slice and lightly steam the courgettes to make them a little less crunchy; pat them dry, scatter generously with fresh basil and dress with a lemony vinaigrette.

Another family favourite is *Courgette Eggah*. Sauté plenty of sliced courgettes in a non-stick pan. Pour on 3–4 lightly beaten eggs for every 1 lb (450 g) of courgettes used and cook until the underside of the eggs begin to set. Sprinkle with cheese and herbs and finish under the grill (broiler). Serve hot or cold.

The best way to make inroads into a glut is preserving. So this year I shall try treating courgettes like marrow, making them into chutneys, pickles and jams with delicious flavourings.

Sometimes broad (fava) and runner beans fail. In other years they leap skywards as though auditioning for the leading vegetable role in Jack and the Beanstalk. By the end of the season they look gross: the pods of broad beans are pot-bellied and blotchy; the skins that encase the beans have turned into leathery jerkins with dirty black thumbnail marks down the seams. Slip off and discard the skins after cooking—they are no pleasure to eat now—and reduce the flesh to a *Broad Bean Purée*. Serve it as a protein-rich vegetable, thin the purée slightly to use as a dip, or thin it considerably (with bacon stock for preference) to make a delicious soup.

The more you cut some types of herb, the more they seem to grow. I use plenty to make glowing herb jellies (page 90) and aromatic herb vinegars, and I even freeze a few. Daily we eat them fresh as a *Herbal Dip*. Coarsely chop lots of parsley and mix with other herbs: some chives, a little dill, tarragon, lemon thyme, chervil—whatever you fancy or have to hand. Serve the greenery with a small bowl of oil and some crusty bread. To eat, hold a bite-size chunk of bread by the crust, thoroughly moisten it with oil and dunk into the herbs. It is one of the simplest and healthiest snacks imaginable.

Soon apples and pears will start to fall from the trees in earnest, thudding softly as they land on the grass, night and day. Bruised and left there they will start to ferment. Blackbirds will lead the feasting and reel about in drunken ecstacy. Wasps will become a menace. The lanes will sprout notices, hastily penned on the back of cardboard boxes and pinned on to gates, announcing that apples, pears, perhaps even quinces, are for sale. In bumper years, people don't even try to sell fruit: they beg the passer-by to stop and take some. I cannot bear not to pick up and use every apple in our garden. I beaver away bottling jellies, jams and chutneys and I freeze large batches of *Stiff Apple Purée* (made as described in Bramley Snow, page 95).

You can also make apple juice, cider and cider vinegar and, of course, a traditional *Fruit Store*. Any cool, dark, fairly dry place, such as an attic, spare room, garage or outhouse will do. But remember that it is only worth storing fruit with good keeping qualities—late varieties are better than early croppers in this respect. The fruit must be perfectly sound, with its stalk intact. Ideally it should be slightly immature, and each piece should be put in a crumpled nest of paper, or otherwise kept from touching its neighbours. Then you must check your stores regularly, ruthlessly removing fruit that shows any sign of deterioration, or the rot will spread like wildfire.

Is it worth all the effort? I think so. Just open the door of a room in which orchard fruits are stored and you are instantly enveloped in a glorious scent, as exuberant in its own way as the smell of freshly mown grass. Sweet ripe apples. They are, for me, the smell of the country in autumn.

BRAMLEY SNOW (PAGE 95)

CONEY WITH BRAMLEYS

Rabbit and apple are again combined in this recipe. But whereas Tanglefoot Rabbit is a very rich dish for special occasions, this is well suited to everyday meals. It is meaty yet low-fat and intriguingly fruity. It is also cheap and easy to cook.

1 rabbit, jointed, or scant 2 lb (1 kg) selected rabbit joints

5–7 fl oz/scant ¾–1 cup (150–170 ml) unsweetened apple juice

1 onion and 1 very large Bramley apple

thyme or rosemary

1–2 tbsp Herb-Garden Jelly (optional; see page 90)

unsalted butter

parsley or croûtons to garnish

Choose a flameproof casserole into which the rabbit joints will fit snugly side by side. Chop the onion very finely and dust the rabbit joints with salt and pepper. Seal and colour the meat and onion, in batches, in ½ oz/1 tbsp (15 g) unsalted butter in a very hot frying pan. Transfer the contents of the pan to the casserole and scatter over them the peeled, cored and finely chopped apple.

"Wash out" the frying pan with the apple juice, stirring the pan base with a wooden spoon to scrape up meaty sediment as the liquid comes to the boil. Pour the apple juice into the casserole. Add a sprig of rosemary or thyme, cover the casserole and cook at 300°F (150°C), mark 2 until the rabbit is perfectly tender; 1½ hours is about right for hutch rabbit, wild rabbit may need 2–2½ hours.

When the rabbit is cooked, carefully lift it out of the casserole and put it on to a warm plate. Cover and keep hot.

Discard the sprig of rosemary or thyme and place the casserole over moderate heat. Beat the contents with a balloon whisk so that the apple disintegrates completely and melts smoothly into the liquid. If necessary simmer for a few minutes, stirring continuously, to give the sauce a good consistency. Season to taste with salt and pepper and add a little Herb-Garden Jelly for piquancy if you like.

Return the rabbit to the casserole, pushing it down into the sauce. This dish will keep hot quite well for 1 hour or so if required. Immediately before serving, scatter a handful of parsley or some croûtons of fried bread over the rabbit. A gratin of potatoes, cooked in the oven alongside the rabbit, goes well with this dish, as do green beans.

SERVES 4–6

S CRUMPY S AUSAGES

There are literally dozens of recipes in which sausages are cooked or finished in a cider sauce. This one is distinguished by its simplicity, and I think it tastes particularly good. It is important to use dessert apples, not cookers, and fresh not dried herbs. Above all, the quality of the sausages matters. It is just not worth using pappy, bland, pink, run-of-the-mill sausages: use good home-made ones for preference.

2 large Cox's apples
1 lb (450 g) sausages
½ pint/1¼ cups (275 ml) or more cider
½ oz/1 tbsp (15 g) unsalted butter
garlic and fresh rosemary or sage

Peel, core and cut the apples into rings. Heat a very large frying pan over a moderate flame. When it is hot, add the butter and swirl to film the entire base of the pan with fat.

Add the apple slices, arranging them in a single layer—if your frying pan is on the small side you may need to cook the apples in batches. Sauté the apples until the flesh is hot, slightly soft and translucent and the surface is streaked with gold. Remove and keep hot.

Put the sausages into the pan and fry them gently, shaking the pan occasionally, until they are pale golden-brown all over. Add one or more garlic cloves to the pan: don't crush them, simply cut them in half. Also add a sprig of fresh herb: either rosemary or sage, or both if you wish.

Pour on the cider and leave to cook, bubbling away gently, until the liquid has almost completely evaporated and the sausages are perfectly cooked right through. Turn the sausages occasionally during this time to encourage even cooking and add more cider to the pan if it begins to dry up too much. You should end up with just a few spoonfuls of syrupy liquid: a mixture of the melted butter, the cider, apple sediment and meaty juices, all delicately flavoured with the garlic and herbs.

Remove the sausages when cooked, and boil down the sauce or deglaze the pan with a few spoonfuls of water if necessary. Season the sauce with salt and pepper, pour it over the sausages and apples and•serve straight away. Mashed potatoes and a watercress salad are the best accompaniments.
SERVES 4

B RAMLEY S NOW

Half the charm of this traditional dish is its light, fruity freshness. It is meant to be tart, so resist the temptation to sweeten it too much. Little biscuits make a good and attractive accompaniment but pouring cream seems to me to be unnecessary and undesirable.

¼ pint/⅔ cup (150 ml) sweet cider
3 lb (1.4 kg) Bramley apples
3 oz/scant ½ cup (75 g) caster (superfine) sugar
3 egg whites
a little chocolate or ground cinnamon to garnish

Measure the cider into a heavy-based saucepan or flameproof casserole. Add the peeled, cored and thinly sliced apples. Cover and cook over very gentle heat until the fruit is quite soft and pulpy. Stir the fruit once or twice during this time. Then remove the lid and continue cooking, stirring frequently, until the fruit is perfectly tender, reduced to a foam and—most importantly—until a good deal of the moisture has been driven off.

Draw the pan away from the heat and stir in the sugar. Leave to cool a little, then process or sieve the fruit to a thick, smooth purée.

Turn the purée into a shallow dish (do not cover) and leave to become cold. It is important that the purée should not be sloppy. Everything up to this stage can usefully be done a day ahead of serving.

Whisk the egg whites until they stand in shiny peaks. Fold in the cold purée and spoon the Bramley Snow into individual dishes or glasses.

Immediately before serving, top with a dusting of ground cinnamon or garnish with curls of chocolate.

To make chocolate curls, either glide a potato peeler over a bar of chocolate to shave off thin curls, or (for more professional results) melt a little chocolate and spread it on a lightly oiled pastry slab; when the chocolate is cold and set, run a knife across it, with the blade angled at 45°, so the chocolate rolls into neat curls as it is cut.
SERVES 8

Warming Soups

Good home-made soup sums up all there is to say about the virtues of country cooking. It is made from the freshest ingredients in season, carefully chosen and simply cooked. It is wholesome, unpretentious and delicious. It is friendly food, made for sharing—and it is sensibly economic of the cook's time and budget. What could be better?

A steaming, fragrantly scented soup tureen is for me one of the most evocative and reassuring sights in the world—synonymous with comfort. For good soup is near-perfect sustenance—food and drink neatly combined in one delicious and easily assimilated form—and I associate the serving of it with relaxed and happy occasions.

Of all soups, those I love best, both to make and to eat, are the ones I call meal-in-a-bowl soups. As the name implies, these are really substantial affairs, so generously afloat with goodies that they are in effect a cross between a soup and a stew, rather like a first course and a main course rolled into one.

Meal-in-a-bowl soups are essentially honest, down-to-earth foods. There is nothing namby-pamby or show-off about them. They are quite simply the soupiest of soups, and their making is rooted in sound commonsense, mindful of practical things and of tasty results.

Meal-in-a-bowl soups are intended to be the main dish of the main meal of the day. They are designed to satisfy healthy appetites made keen by fresh country air and they are deliberately generous in quantity (each of the recipes given here allows for large first helpings and for second helpings too). Most make plentiful use of fresh vegetables in season, and they often include cereals or pulses as well, but the use of meat is usually very sparing indeed. This is in line with traditional cottage economy, of course, and coincidentally it makes for healthy, well balanced eating.

These soups are aggreeably easy on the cook. They are relatively inexpensive and pretty straight-forward. No ultra-precise weighing of ingredients, no split-second timing, no tricky cooking tech-niques are involved. They are the sort of dishes which can be cooked easily while chatting to members of the family who may gather round to share the cosy warmth of the kitchen, and who may be willing to lend a hand with chopping the veg-etables, laying the table or whatever. Last, but by no means least from the cook's point of view, most meal-in-a-bowl soups are blessedly good-tempered. The antithesis of a soufflé, they do not insist on being eaten the moment they are cooked. What is more, leftovers (should there ever be any) can usually be saved for reheating and serving again on another day without any noticeable loss of quality.

Meal-in-a-bowl soups are just the thing for a restorative lunch at the end of a raw morning if you've been up and out for what seems like hours, and feel you deserve something more substantial and warming than the ubiquitous ploughman's bread, pickle and cheese. Serving these very special soups in the evening is even better. They are lovely for family suppers and I find them perfect for sharing with friends when you want to relax and enjoy a cosy supper party (gathered round the fireside or a candlelit kitchen table) rather than face the fuss and formality of a full-scale dinner party.

Friends will feel treated if you accompany the soup with two or more sorts of bread—say hot garlic bread and a granary loaf. Nearly all shop-bought loaves are improved by heating them through in the oven just before serving: this crisps the crust and warms the crumb, giving the bread a "fresh-baked" aroma. Even more appetising of course is genuine, fresh bread that you've made yourself (see pages 30–41).

Another way to create a little sense of occasion is to offer a choice of butters to go with the breads. Plain salted or unsalted butter takes on party status if stamped into pretty shapes with a traditional butter mould or if patted and rolled into balls with old-fashioned "scotch hands".

Flavoured butters are fun to make and appealing. Don't worry if you make too much: leftover flavoured butters make tasty garnishes for grilled (broiled) meats and fish; they are glorious melted over pasta and steamed vegetables; and they make a pleasant change with baked potatoes.

Meal-in-a-bowl soups are splendid and filling, like a first course and a main course rolled into one. Nothing should be served beforehand and very little needs to be served afterwards. I suggest a crisp green salad and cheese (excellent served simultaneously, as they often are in France and Italy) and then perhaps a light pudding. Something sweet is far from essential, but nice for a party. I stress the word light because a rich or heavy dessert would be quite inappropriate. All that is needed to round off the meal admirably is a tiny sweet afterthought—little helpings of, say, apple snow or fresh lemon sorbet.

Here are quick reminders of how to make hot garlic bread and various flavoured butters:

HOT GARLIC BREAD

Crush 3 garlic cloves with ½ tsp salt and beat to a cream with 4 oz/1 stick (115 g) softened butter. Cut a French or Vienna loaf into slices without cutting through the base. Fan out the slices and spread one side of each slice generously with garlic butter. Press the loaf together again, wrap it in foil and place it on a baking sheet. Bake in a fairly hot oven for about 20 minutes unwrapping the top of the foil for the last 5 minutes to crisp the crust.

FLAVOURED BUTTERS

Use butter at room temperature. Put it into a soup plate. Add your chosen flavouring (see below) and mash with a fork until smoothly blended. Pack the flavoured butter into a small pot, cover it and refrigerate it briefly before serving.

Herb butter: 2–3 tbsp chopped fresh herbs per 2 oz/½ stick (50 g) butter. A mixture of chives and parsley goes well with most pulse and vegetable soups; include a little dill to accompany fish soups, or tarragon for chicken, or thyme for pork and game.

Anchovy butter: 4 anchovy fillets, pounded to a paste with mortar and pestle, or a few drops of anchovy essence per 2 oz/½ stick (50 g) butter.

Devilled butter: 1 tsp or more mustard plus Worcestershire sauce to taste and a dash of cayenne pepper per 2 oz/½ stick (50 g) butter.

Citrus butter: 1 tsp finely grated zest plus 2 tsp freshly squeezed juice per 2 oz/½ stick (50 g) butter.

Paprika butter: 1 tbsp sweet Hungarian paprika plus 2 tsp minced onion per 2 oz/½ stick (50 g) butter.

Blue-cheese butter: 1–1¼ parts Dolcelatte or other blue cheese to 2 parts butter, plus a squeeze of lemon juice.

Mustard butter: 2 tsp wholegrain mustard, preferably a mild variety made with honey, per 2 oz/½ stick (50 g) butter. This goes particularly well with Rabbit-In-A-Bowl soup, page 101.

Sesame butter: 1–2 tbsp sesame seeds, lightly toasted until pale brown and nutty, per 2 oz/½ stick (50 g) butter.

KILKENNY CREAM

What makes this essentially simple dish so satisfying is the way the ingredients complement each other. Success depends on everything being top quality and beautifully fresh; nothing should be omitted and nothing substituted. Skimmed milk and a low-fat alternative to butter may make sense sometimes—but not for this recipe.

1½ lb (700 g) onions
1 lb (450 g) potatoes
butter
dried tarragon and a bay leaf
2½ pints/6¼ cups (1.4 litres) milk
about 6–8 oz (200 g) streaky bacon
4 eggs
good crusty bread
3 large bunches watercress

Slice the onions very thinly and dice the potatoes.

Melt 4 oz/1 stick (125 g) butter in a large heavy-based pan. Stir in the onion, cover the pan and sweat the onion very gently for 15–20 minutes until it is beautifully soft and translucent.

Add the potatoes to the pan and stir for a minute or so to coat all over with fat. Add ½ tsp dried tarragon, the bay leaf and a very generous seasoning of salt and pepper.

Reserve the top of the milk. Pour the rest of the milk into the soup pan and bring to simmering point. Give the ingredients a good stir, half cover the pan and leave to simmer very gently indeed until the potatoes are tender, just stirring the ingredients occasionally as they cook. Discard the bay leaf and reduce the soup to a smooth purée. (Everything up to this stage can be done well ahead of serving.)

Shortly before serving, cut the bacon into snippets and fry until crisp. Soft boil the eggs, shell them and put them into warmed soup plates. Reheat the soup very carefully, stirring frequently to prevent sticking. Check seasoning, then pour the soup into a warmed tureen or ladle it directly into the plates. Swirl with the top of the milk and sprinkle with the bacon snippets. Serve accompanied by plenty of open watercress sandwiches: thick slices of fresh bread, generously buttered and piled high with peppery crisp watercress.
SERVES 4

KILKENNY CREAM (PAGE 97)

RISI E BISI

This delicately flavoured soup is particularly soothing. It's just what I need when I am feeling fraught and weary. Unusually for a meal-in-a-bowl soup, it is not thick with fresh vegetables but is made from standard larder cupboard items. This makes it a great standby for emergencies.

1 large onion
2 oz/½ stick (50 g) butter
10 oz/scant 1½ cups (275 g) arborio rice
2¼ pints/5⅔ cups (1.25 litres) good poultry, veal or fish stock
1 × 14 oz (400 g) can of petits pois
freshly grated Parmesan cheese
fresh chopped parsley

Chop the onion finely. Cook it in half the butter in a heavy-based pan until slightly softened and translucent. Add the rice and cook, stirring, for 1 or 2 minutes until each grain glistens with fat. Season with a good grinding of pepper.

Pour on a generous ½ pint/1¼ cups (300 ml) of the piping-hot stock and let the rice cook at a moderate bubble, without a lid, until most of the liquid has been absorbed. Stir the rice occasionally as it cooks to prevent it sticking to the pan base.

Pour on the rest of the boiling hot stock and continue cooking for about 12 minutes until the rice is tender but still has a little bite to it. Don't cover the pan during this time, but stir the rice every now and again. If the liquid begins to dry up before the rice is ready, add another ladleful or two of hot stock—the aim is to produce a risotto bathed in a little broth.

When the rice is ready, add the peas and their liquid, the rest of the butter and 1 oz/2 tbsp (25 g) grated Parmesan, in that order. Continue cooking gently, just long enough to melt the butter and cheese, by which time the peas should be heated through.

Stir well and check seasoning. Serve very hot, handing round at the table a bowl of fresh chopped parsley and another of grated Parmesan so that everyone can help themselves.
SERVES 4

BEANFEAST WITH YOGHURT

A healthy soup and excellent for a party. Serve it with pitta bread and hand round a big bowl of creamy yoghurt (home-made or Greek strained yoghurt) to be added according to taste. A second garnishing ingredient is far from essential but may also be handed round at table if wished: miniature spiced meatballs, toasted pumpkin seeds, chopped hard-boiled eggs, and slivers of stir-fried chicken are all good choices. I sometimes make a big batch of this soup and serve it on successive days, offering a different garnish on each occasion for the sake of variety.

3 oz/scant ½ cup (75 g) chick-peas
3 oz/½ cup (75 g) red kidney beans
3 tbsp olive or sunflower oil
2 large onions
2 garlic cloves
turmeric, cinnamon and dried mint
5 pints/3 quarts (2.8 litres) light stock
1 scant tsp dried mint
6 oz/scant 1 cup (175 g) whole green lentils
6 oz/1 cup (175 g) brown rice
2 large bunches of watercress
½ pint/1¼ cups (330 ml) creamy yoghurt

Soak the chick-peas and kidney beans in plenty of cold water overnight. Drain them the next day. Cover with fresh cold water, boil for 10 minutes and drain again.

Warm the oil in a large heavy-based pan. Stir in the chopped onions. Add the crushed garlic, a well-rounded tsp each of turmeric and ground cinnamon. Stir again.

Add the chick-peas and kidney beans, the stock, a scant tsp dried mint and lots of pepper—but no salt. Cover and simmer gently for 35 minutes. Stir in the lentils and rice. Cover and simmer for 35 minutes more or until pulses and rice are tender.

Season with salt and add extra spices and flavourings to taste. Add the watercress (chopped to tiny green flecks in a blender or food processor) and cook for just a few minutes more. Put the yoghurt into a bowl and beat into it a ladleful of the hot soup liquid, then beat the contents of the bowl into the soup pan. Heat through gently (do not boil or the yoghurt may curdle) and serve.
SERVES 6

RABBIT-IN-A-BOWL

This very homely soup is made in the old-fashioned farmhouse way—cooked very slowly in a gentle oven. It is a method worth using whatever sort of stove you have because it is so effortless and because it produces such good results, tenderising meats and beans and blending their flavours deliciously.

8–10 oz/scant 1⅓ cups (about 250 g) flageolet beans or white haricot beans
6 oz (175 g) belly of pork (salt pork), boneless weight
4 small rabbit joints, or 8 oz (255 g) boneless rabbit
4 garlic cloves
dried thyme and oregano
2 lemons and plenty of fresh parsley
1 lb (450 g) leeks
¼ pint/⅔ cup (150 ml) dry cider
2 pints/5 cups (1.1 litres) cold stock

Soak the beans overnight. Rinse and drain them. Chop the meats into generous bite-size pieces and put into a casserole. Add 3 crushed garlic cloves, a scant tsp of thyme and ½ tsp oregano, a little finely grated lemon zest and plenty of pepper—but no salt. Stir to mix well.

Cover the meats with thickly sliced leeks (tender green parts as well as white), then the drained beans. Pour on the juice of half a lemon, the cider and the stock (the stock should be cold, not hot).

Cover the casserole and put it into the oven to cook slowly at 250–300°F (140–150°C), mark 1–2 for about 5 hours until the beans are really soft and the meats are meltingly tender. It won't come to any harm if left to cook for a bit longer.

Stir well, season generously with salt and add extra flavourings to taste just before serving. Finally, garnish with gremolata. To make this, chop one fat garlic clove very finely and mix it with the finely grated zest of the lemon and 4–5 tbsp fresh chopped parsley.

SERVES 4

SAVOY POTAGE

Plain Potato Cakes (see recipe on page 105) make a particularly good accompaniment to this splendid soup in which sweet chestnuts, spices and sausages imbue the humble cabbage with their richness. Any firm-hearted green cabbage—Savoy, January King or Primo—can be used. The better the stock, the better the soup.

1½ oz (40 g) dried chestnuts
3 onions
2 oz/½ stick (50 g) butter
¾ tsp caraway seeds
3½ pints/8¾ cups (2 litres) good poultry or ham stock
Savoy cabbage, weighing about 3 lb (1.4 kg)
12 oz (350 g) spicy, cured sausages, such as cabanos or chorizio
½ pint/1¼ cups (275 ml) soured cream or creamy home-made yoghurt or Greek strained yoghurt
1 tbsp sweet Hungarian paprika

Soak the dried chestnuts overnight in a bowl of warm water. Drain them the next day and chop finely.

Sweat the onions in the butter in a covered pan over low heat for about 10 minutes, stirring occasionally. Gently bruise the caraway with mortar and pestle. Add it and the chestnuts to the pan. Pour on the stock and bring to simmering point. Cover and cook for about 10 minutes.

Quarter the cabbage. Discard the stalk and finely shred (2¼ lb) 1 kg of the leaves. Stir the shredded cabbage into the pan. Cut the sausages into thin slices and add them to the pan.

Cook gently just long enough for the cabbage to become tender yet still retain a little bite, and for the sausages to heat through. Check the soup for seasoning and adjust to taste.

Beat the soured cream or yoghurt in a cup with the sweet Hungarian paprika. Gently swirl and float the spicy cream on top of the soup immediately before serving.

SERVES 6

MUSSEL SOUP

The best way to eat this is fisherman fashion—tipping the mussels from shell to mouth with your fingers, then spooning up the fragrant tomato-rice broth. Give each person a napkin large enough to tie round their neck and a fingerbowl of warm water for rinsing sticky fingers.

8 lb (4.5 litres) mussels
4 tbsp olive oil
1 lb (450 g) onions and 2 fat garlic cloves
6 oz/scant 1 cup (175 g) long-grain rice
a few saffron strands, pounded with mortar and pestle
    and soaked in $\frac{1}{2}$ pint/1$\frac{1}{4}$ cups (250 ml) water
2 × 14 oz (400 g) cans tomatoes
$\frac{1}{2}$ pint/1$\frac{1}{4}$ cups (250 ml) dry white wine

Thoroughly scrub the mussels and wash them in several changes of cold, salted water. Discard any that are damaged or refuse to shut tightly when tapped sharply.

Warm the oil in a large saucepan. Add the onions (peeled, very thinly sliced and pushed into rings) and the chopped garlic. Soften gently for a few minutes, then add the rice and stir for 2–3 minutes until the grains are transparent.

Add the saffron strands plus the liquid they have been soaking in, the roughly chopped tomatoes and their liquid and bring to the boil, stirring. Cover tightly and cook very gently for about 15 minutes until the rice is tender and has absorbed most of the liquid.

Unless you have a really large pan it is best to cook the mussels in two batches. Bring the wine to simmering point, add the mussels, cover and cook over fierce heat for a minute or two to steam the shells open. Shake the pan occasionally so that the steam can circulate easily. Then reduce the heat and simmer for a further 2–3 minutes.

Turn the contents of the mussel pan into a colander placed over a large bowl. Throw away any mussels that have not opened. Remove empty half shells and place the cooked mussels in a warmed soup tureen.

Strain the mussel liquor into the rice pan, passing it through a butter-muslin-lined sieve to extract any grit. Bring broth and rice gently back to simmering point and check seasoning before pouring the soup over the mussels.

SERVES 4

CHICKEN BONNE FEMME

I first made this soup to use up leftovers from a Sunday lunch (scraps of roast chicken, gravy and giblet stock), ekeing them out with fresh vegetables from the garden when friends turned up unexpectedly and my larder was almost bare. It is now a great family favourite and I always buy a really big chicken for roasting to be sure there will be enough leftovers to make this soup. A lot of meat is unnecessary but good home-made stock and rich gravy are vital. The recipe works equally well using turkey.

1$\frac{1}{2}$ lb (700 g) potatoes
1$\frac{1}{2}$ lb (700 g) leeks
$\frac{1}{2}$ lb (250 g) carrots
2 oz/$\frac{1}{4}$ cup (50 g) fat scraped from the top of chicken
    gravy, or butter
sugar and a little dried tarragon
chicken gravy and chicken stock
6–8 oz (200–250 g) cooked chicken meat, skinned and
    boned weight
fresh parsley

Cut the potatoes into chunks, peeling them first if you wish. Slice the leeks fairly thickly, green parts as well as white, and slice the carrots thinly.

Warm the fat in a large saucepan or flameproof casserole placed over a low heat. Add the vegetables and stir to coat them all over with fat. Cover the pan and cook gently for 6 or 7 minutes, just stirring the vegetables occasionally.

Add a generous pinch each of sugar and dried tarragon, a little salt and a good grinding of black pepper.

Pour on the gravy plus enough stock to make a total 2$\frac{1}{2}$ pints/6$\frac{1}{4}$ cups (1.4 litres) of liquid. Bring to the boil and give a good stir. Cover the pan and simmer gently until the vegetables are half cooked. Then add the chicken meat, cut into slivers, and continue simmering gently until the vegetables are cooked to your liking and the chicken is thoroughly heated through.

Just before serving, check and adjust seasoning to taste and thin the broth with extra stock if you want a more liquid soup. Stir in several spoonfuls of chopped fresh parsley—and add a small handful of crisp fried bread croûtons (lightly flavoured with garlic) if liked.

SERVES 4

CHICKEN BONNE FEMME

Hunter's Homecoming with Chive Toasts

Dark and rich, this is wonderfully warming. It is best (and cheapest) made in autumn using freshly picked field mushrooms but very good made using the large, flat, cultivated mushrooms now available all year round at good greengrocers. Do not use cap or button mushrooms: both types lack sufficient colour and flavour. Unless you own an extremely large saucepan or flameproof casserole, it is impractical to try to make this soup in larger quantities than I give here—because raw, chopped mushrooms are so bulky at the beginning of cooking.

1½ lb (700 g) flat, dark, velvety gilled mushrooms
2 onions
6 lamb's kidneys
coriander seeds and cumin seeds
3 oz/¾ stick (75 g) butter
2 tbsp flour
2 pints/5 cups (1.1 litres) light stock
3 tbsp Madeira
3–4 tbsp creamy yoghurt (home-made or Greek-strained yoghurt)

For the chive toasts:
1 small Bloomer loaf
a little olive oil
low-fat soft fresh cheese (or curd or cream cheese if you prefer)
fresh chopped chives or spring onions (scallions)

Chop the mushrooms into quite small pieces, and chop the onions finely. Skin, halve and core the kidneys and slice them thinly. Put 2 tsp coriander seeds and ½ tsp cumin seeds into a mortar and bruise and lightly crush them with a pestle.

Put the spices into a very large flameproof casserole or heavy-based pan and place over low heat. When the spices smell aromatic, add a small piece of butter. As soon as the butter is very hot, add the kidneys and cook very briefly, stirring and turning just long enough to colour the meat. On no account fry long or hard or the kidney will become tough and lose its delicate flavour. Remove the kidney from the casserole and reserve it on a plate.

Add another knob of butter to the pan and cook the onions gently for 5 minutes. Then increase the heat and add the rest of the butter. When the butter foam begins to die down, add the mushrooms. Cook them, stirring continuously, for at least 5 minutes until slightly softened and reduced in bulk.

Sprinkle on the flour and stir it in. Pour on the hot stock and bring to simmering point, stirring all the while. Add the Madeira, a little salt and a good grinding of black pepper and leave to simmer, without a lid, for 5 minutes.

Draw the pan away from the heat and transfer most of the mushrooms to a food processor or blender, fishing them out of the soup pan with a slotted spoon. Add a little of the soup liquid and reduce to a black flecked purée.

Return the purée to the soup pan, bring back to simmering point and check seasoning. Just before serving, add the reserved kidneys and heat through very gently. Serve in a very hot soup tureen, garnished with swirls of yoghurt, and hand round lots of chive toasts.

To make the chive toasts (which can be prepared well ahead), first cut the bread into thick slices, brush lightly on both sides with a little olive oil and toast under the grill (broiler) until golden. Cool the toasts on a cake rack, then spread one side of each generously with low-fat soft fresh cheese and garnish with a good sprinkling of fresh chopped chives (or finely chopped spring onions if chives are unavailable).
SERVES 4

COOK'S NOTEBOOK

I love having friends to stay for the weekend, because this prolongs the sharing of good company and offers a real chance to catch up fully on each other's news and views. The only trouble is that many city folk appear, not unnaturally, to like to visit their country friends in the height of summer when it's not necessary to get the inside of their cars dirty with disgracefully muddy wellingtons.

In winter it may be necessary to woo visitors from town by laying on generously all the comforts of the country. No matter how effective your central heating, always add a log fire. This is something money cannot buy in big cities and it never fails to please.

Grapefruit and muesli are the order of the day for weekday breakfasts in this health-conscious age, and I certainly subscribe to and applaud the general trend towards healthier eating. But most of us let our hair down a little at weekends, if only to the extent of allowing ourselves a croissant instead of the usual slice of wholemeal toast, and I see nothing wrong in indulging very occasionally.

My idea of a once-in-a-blue-moon treat is a totally unhurried, slap-up British breakfast, with nobody expected to be on parade at a fixed hour, but free to appear when they wish, and to come dressing-gowned if they want to.

Home-made marmalade and honey in the comb are musts. So are the freshest of fresh free-range eggs, which can be boiled to order as breakfasters appear. There are bowls of oatmeal porridge and a jug of freshly squeezed juice.

There might be sizzling rashers of bacon and herb-flavoured sausages (guaranteed to impress if home-made), or an old-fashioned breakfast dish such as *Devilled Kidneys*. The secret of this is to grill (broil) the kidneys only briefly and to make the devilled butter very devilish: I allow 2 tsp mustard powder, 1½ tsp Worcestershire sauce and a good shake each of anchovy essence, cayenne pepper, Harvey's sauce and mushroom ketchup for every 1½ oz/scant ½ stick (40 g) of butter.

Kedgeree is another traditional breakfast favourite, and particularly delicious is the version I call *Fresh Herb Kedgeree*. This is made using brown rice, instead of white, and with quite a bit less smoked haddock and eggs than usual. Instead, it is brilliantly flavoured and coloured with lavish quantities of fresh chopped parsley and chives, and enriched with a knob of butter.

Cooks who dislike cooking early in the day will find salvation in *Jugged Kippers*, surely the most civilised fish dish in the world as it involves no cooking in the accepted sense of the word, and leaves no lingering fishy smells. Stand kippers in a tall jug, pour on enough boiling water to immerse the fish, cover the jug with a dome of foil and leave for 5–6 minutes before draining and serving.

Equally effortless, and greatly favoured by cooks who own Agas, are oven-cooked dishes like baked eggs and *Breakfast Mushrooms on Toast*. To make the latter, lightly butter slices of bread on both sides and lay them side by side on a baking tray. Bake in a fairly hot oven for about 15 minutes until the bread begins to frizzle and turn pale gold. Cover the bread with flat shaggy mushrooms, laid gill side up. Season well with salt and pepper, dot with very thin flakes of butter and bake for about 15 minutes until the mushrooms are bubbling hot.

Another breakfast dish I remember very vividly from my childhood is *Potato Cakes*. These are an Irish speciality, and the Irish are wizards with potatoes. To make a good batch you need 1 lb (450 g) mashed potatoes and ¾ lb/scant 2½ cups (325 g) self-raising flour. Put the mashed potatoes—which must be cold—into a mixing bowl and break up any large lumps with your fingertips. Add the flour and plenty of salt and freshly ground black pepper, and stir or rub the ingredients to get them fairly well blended. Add 2 lightly beaten eggs and 3 oz/¾ stick (75 g) barely melted butter or bacon fat, and beat vigorously with a wooden spoon until everything is well blended and forms a smooth dough. Knead lightly, working in more flour as necessary if the dough is too soft to handle easily—a lot depends on how moist the mashed potatoes are.

Roll the dough out to about ¼ inch (6 mm) thick and cut it into rounds, using a scone cutter for small potato cakes or an upturned cup for big potato cakes. Shallow fry in batches, in a mixture of butter and oil, over medium heat until hot, crisp and golden—about 3 minutes on each side.

Potato cakes are wonderful for breakfast with rashers of fat streaky bacon or grilled tomatoes, or both. They are also excellent for supper.

WINTER

In Winter we relish the fruits of this year's harvest and plan the next, roasting chestnuts as we pour over the seedsmen's catalogues, stirring the Christmas pudding and making a wish.

Winter Vegetables

The first frosts herald the end of sweet summer vegetables. Produce like tomatoes, peas and tender-leafed butterhead lettuce are constitutionally just too delicate to survive the chill. Now is the time when root vegetables come to the fore. They are the toughies of the vegetable world, born survivors, robust enough to withstand wind, rain and cold in the field. They are just right, too, for helping cooks and their families to stoke up with the nutritional comfort and warmth needed to face the rigours of winter.

I use the word roots loosely; meaning true root vegetables (like carrots, parsnips, salsify, scorzonera, beetroot, turnips, swedes and celeriac), as well as bulbs (like onions), tubers (like potatoes and Jerusalem artichokes), and stem vegetables such as leeks and celery. I count these last as underground vegetables in that protective walls of earth are built up around them as they grow.

I welcome the return of the root vegetable season for the sense of security that follows in its wake. Plaiting strings of onion and garlic is therapeutic and the traditional task of clamping carrots and parsnips is surely symbolic of safely battening down the hatches in preparation for the onslaught of winter. I also welcome the return to the root vegetable season because it signals a return to some of our best-loved country cooking—good, honest dishes that are easy to cook and easy to eat, as reassuringly familiar as old friends: thick soups and no-nonsense stews, substantial pilaffs and tasty rich beanpots.

The vivid colours and flavours of root vegetables, or "pot herbs" as they used to be called, offer a brilliant means of enlivening plain dishes of pulses or grains—and in this role roots are invaluable vegetarian fare. Root vegetables are also wonderful for ekeing out frugal quantities of meat. Last but by no means least, they can be superb as vegetable dishes pure and simple. Break away from the boring boiled-and-buttered routine and you will find that roots take on a new lease of life: they make much more interesting accompaniments to main courses, and often deserve to be served as a first course.

One of the heartening things about the current revival of interest in all things to do with the countryside is rediscovered pride in some of our traditional vegetables. Old-fashioned favourites like salsify and scorzonera are enjoying a well deserved renaissance. Forgotten for far too long, now they are beginning to flourish again—available for green-fingered folk to grow in garden or allotment and for non-gardeners to buy in good greengrocers and enlightened supermarkets.

SALSIFY AND SCORZONERA

The old nickname for salsify is "vegetable oyster", which suggests a faint taste of the sea. I can't detect any ozone myself, any more than I can hear the sea when I put a shell to my ear. But salsify most certainly is very delicious and delicate— and connoisseurs of these succulent roots rate scorzonera (salsify's black-skinned cousin) even more highly. Both vegetables should be cooked whole and very gently to prevent flavour leaching out. The skin is tough and needs to be peeled away *after* cooking.

JERUSALEM ARTICHOKE

The Jerusalem artichoke is another vegetable that is well worth growing. In fact it is an irrepressible plant, rampaging over the garden happily once it has a foothold. The lumpy, bumpy, whiskery tubers look far from special when you dig them up, but cut a Jerusalem artichoke open and you will find translucent flesh with a mother-of-pearl sheen. The flavour is equally beautiful: delicately nutty and crisp when raw, faintly earthy and intriguingly smoky when cooked.

KOHLRABI

I confess I find little pleasure in cooking or eating swedes and winter turnips. The first baby turnips of summer, with their beguiling mauve and white sweet-pea colouring and their light peppery taste, are a different story—and so is kohlrabi. Strictly speaking kohlrabi is not a root, it is a swollen stem, but its bulbous appearance and the fact that it has a not-too-aggressive turnip flavour mean it makes an agreeable alternative to winter turnips and swedes in stews and similar recipes. It also makes good bortsch-type soups when teamed with beetroot. As a vegetable plain and simple, I like it steamed until just tender then finished with a light cream or cheese or garlicky tomato sauce. Save young kohlrabi leaves, and young beetroot leaves too. They can be cooked like greens.

BEETROOT, PARSNIP AND CARROT

I love hot, freshly cooked beetroot (beets). Its sweet earthy taste is a glorious revelation after the ghastly experience of shop-bought ready-cooked beetroot drowned in crude malt vinegar. In earlier times, when sugar was a scarce and expensive luxury, beetroot was primarily prized for its sweetness. Parsnips and carrots were popular for the same reason and all three were regularly used in making puddings and cakes.

CELERIAC

This is one of my favourite vegetables. It more or less disappeared from the British scene for many years, but now, I am glad to say, it is fast returning to favour with cooks and gardeners alike. Celeriac (celery root) looks unprepossessing but makes exquisite eating, having a nutty-sweet celery flavour—a treat to eat raw or cooked. It is one of the few vegetables to which the maxim "small is beautiful" does not apply. Specimens quite a lot bigger than coconuts and twice as ugly have magnificent flavour and texture. The contorted whorls of rootlets that wrap themselves octopus-fashion all around celeriac mean this is a vegetable which must be peeled as well as scrubbed. As with Jerusalem artichokes, celeriac flesh discolours when exposed to air; so unless it is to be used instantly, it is a good idea to drop celeriac into a bowl of acidulated water as soon as prepared, that is to say a bowl of water to which a little vinegar or lemon has been added.

Like all other sorts of vegetables, roots taste best and contain most vitamins if eaten within hours of picking, but roots retain their freshness far better and far longer than tender summer vegetables. Whereas a lettuce will flag limply within hours, irrevocably drained of all vitality, maincrop potatoes can be stored in a cool dark place for several weeks.

Root vegetables must, of course, be in prime condition when harvested if they are to make good eating. If left to grow on to OAP status their texture will become coarse and fibrous, their flavour faded or crude. Leeks as stout as marble pillars are no pleasure to eat; gargantuan parsnips and carrots develop disagreeably woody cores; kohlrabi is distasteful if allowed to grow as large as a tennis ball; and beetroots taste sweetest if no bigger than ping-pong balls.

Always check that the skins of root vegetables are taut and smooth. The flesh underneath should feel firm, never flabby. If a vegetable feels or looks tired and unhappy, no amount of cossetting by the cook will revive it. Store only the very best, checking that they are free from cuts made during lifting and not marred by other blemishes. Leave foliage intact if possible and a little earth clinging to root whiskers to help preserve moisture and freshness. Trimming a vegetable always reduces its life expectancy—so spare the knife until just before cooking.

ORIENTAL CARROTS

Maincrop carrots are much richer in flavour than the little finger carrots of early summer, and cooking them this way imbues them with a hint of the exotic. First-class fruity olive oil is an important ingredient here. This dish reheats well and partners plain roast or grilled poultry nicely. It also makes an admirable meatless main course: stir in a very generous handful of well toasted almonds just before serving and accompany with brown rice.

generous 1 lb (500 g) carrots
generous $\frac{1}{2}$ lb (250 g) onions
4 tbsp fruity flavoured olive oil
1 large orange
3 oz/$\frac{1}{2}$ cup (75 g) large, seeded raisins

You will need a large heavy-based saucepan for this dish, or preferably a flameproof casserole that can be brought from the kitchen to the dining table. Peel the onions and slice them. Scrub the carrots, or peel them if you insist, and slice them. Keep the two vegetables separate at this stage.

Warm the saucepan or casserole over moderately low heat. Add the olive oil, and when it is warm and smelling sweet, add the onions. Cover and shake the pan vigorously to film the onions all over with the oil. Place the pan back over the heat and cook gently for 2–3 minutes.

Add the carrots, cover and shake the pan again to encourage even distribution of the oil, then add a little salt and a good grinding of pepper, and pour on the freshly squeezed juice of the orange. Cover the pan tightly; if the pan has an ill-fitting lid place a sheet of foil between the pan and the lid to ensure a good seal.

Cook the vegetables over the lowest possible heat for 30 minutes, just shaking the pan and turning the ingredients occasionally.

Add the raisins and continue cooking as before for another 30 minutes or more. It will take at least 1 hour in total for the vegetables to become beautifully tender.

Take care not to let the vegetables brown or to let the pan burn dry—add a splash of water if necessary. The vegetables should absorb most of the oil and orange juice during cooking. If there is more than a spoonful or so of liquid left in the pan at the end of cooking time, remove the lid and cook for a few minutes more until it evaporates.

When ready to serve, season the vegetables with more salt and pepper to taste and add a tiny pinch of orange zest if you want to heighten the fruity element of the dish.

SERVES 4–6

BRAISED CELERY WITH ANCHOVY SAUCE

This is a recipe for those who love anchovies—exceedingly rich and very delicious. It makes a wonderfully ritzy appetiser to serve before a light main course, with masses of bread to mop up every last drop of the sauce. Or it can be served as a vegetable accompaniment to very plainly cooked foods, such as steamed or poached chicken or fish. For a straightforward dish of braised celery, simply omit the anchovy cream sauce.

3 large, firm, tightly packed heads of celery
1½ oz/3 tbsp (40 g) butter
celery salt
3 tbsp stock plus 1 tbsp dry white
  vermouth
1 can anchovy fillets
¼ pint/⅔ cup (150 ml) double (heavy) cream
fresh parsley, chopped
a handful of black (ripe) olives

Trim the roots and tops to give fine fat heads of celery 7–8 inches (18–20 cm) long. Scrape away any stringy threads from the outer sticks of each head and wash well under a cold tap. Then stand the whole heads upside-down in a tall jug of cold water for 10 minutes. Blanch the celery by simmering it gently for 12 minutes in salted water. Drain very thoroughly and, when cool enough to handle, cut each head in half lengthways and pat dry.

Lay the celery pieces in a single layer in a buttered gratin or baking dish. Dot with the remaining butter, sprinkle with salt, pepper and celery salt and pour on the stock and vermouth.

Lay a piece of buttered greaseproof paper directly on top of the vegetables. Braise for 1 hour at 350°F (180°C), mark 4. Turn the celery over, baste it and continue braising—without the paper this time—for 25 minutes more.

Put the anchovies and their oil into a heavy-based saucepan and cook over very low heat, crushing the anchovies with a wooden spoon until they disintegrate into the oil. Pour on any juices remaining in the celery dish, then the cream. Let the mixture bubble up, become hot and well blended.

Continue cooking until the sauce is very thick indeed and perfectly smooth. Season it with pepper and pour it over the celery. (Braised celery, with or without the anchovy sauce, can be covered with foil and kept hot in a low oven for at least 30 minutes between cooking and serving. Both versions also reheat well from cold.) For extra colour and flavour, garnish the dish with chopped fresh parsley and a few olives immediately before serving.
SERVES 4–6

NUTTY SPICED BEETROOT

This recipe is a simple and very effective alternative to the usual practice of serving hot boiled beetroot in a white sauce. The toasted nuts and spices come as a surprise yet seem a natural complement to the earthy sweetness of beetroot. If the beetroot are not as small as you would wish, halve or quarter them when you strip off the skins after preliminary cooking. A good vegetable to serve with roast beef or lamb.

12 small fresh beetroot (beets), weighing about 1¾ lb
  (800 g) in total
16 hazelnut kernels
generous 1 tbsp sesame seeds
scant 1 tsp cumin seeds
2 tsp coriander seeds
1–2 tbsp olive oil

Choose the beetroot carefully—it is important that the skins are not broken in any places and they should have at least ½ inch (1 cm) of root and stalk attached. If they are trimmed too neatly, or if the skin is so much as grazed, the gloriously coloured juices of the beets will "bleed" during cooking.

Wash the beetroot but do not peel them. Cook them until tender—boiling, steaming or baking them as you wish. As soon as cool enough to handle, strip off the skins and trim root and stalk.

While the beetroot is cooking, toast the hazelnuts. Cook them in a frying pan without any fat, over medium heat, until they are aromatic and the papery skins are sufficiently brown to rub off easily. Take the hazelnuts out of the pan and set aside.

Reduce heat to low and add the sesame, cumin and coriander seeds to the pan. Toast, shaking the pan fairly frequently, until the seeds are deliciously aromatic. The point of this operation is to intensify the flavours and fragrance of nuts, seeds and spices.

Rub the skins off the hazelnuts. Then put the nuts, seeds and spices into an electric coffee mill or a food processor or blender and reduce to a fairly coarse powder. Season the mixture generously with salt and pepper.

Warm the olive oil in the frying pan. Add the cooked, peeled and trimmed beetroot and sprinkle the spicy mixture on top. Cook gently, just shaking the pan and turning the beetroot occasionally, for a few minutes until the beetroot are thoroughly hot again and dusted all over with a coating of aromatic spicy mixture. Serve immediately.
SERVES 6

FRIED CELERIAC WITH APPLES AND WALNUTS

The combination of raw celeriac and raw apple is so good in salads that I thought I would try a cooked version. The result is every bit as delicious but somehow more delicate, perhaps because it is unexpected. Two things are important to success: use very little butter and cook the ingredients briefly. If the ingredients are allowed to become greasy or soggy all the charm of the dish will be lost.

1½ lb (700 g) prepared weight celeriac (celery root)
2 Cox's apples, weighing a total 8–10 oz (225–275 g)
1 lemon or a little vinegar
½ oz/1 tbsp (15 g) unsalted butter
2 oz/½ cup (50 g) walnut pieces

You will need a large celeriac root, or perhaps even two, to produce the required weight of flesh. Peel away the outside; scoop out and discard the slightly woolly centre. Cut the firm white flesh into ½ inch (1.5 cm) dice, or slightly larger.

Drop the dice as soon as prepared into a bowl of cold water to which 1–2 tbsp lemon juice or vinegar have been added.

Drain and cook the celeriac in fast-boiling water for 2 minutes only—just long enough for the celeriac to lose its raw qualities. Drain again, cool slightly and pat dry.

While it cools, quickly peel and core the apples and cut them into dice about the same size as the celeriac.

Warm a large non stick frying pan. Melt the butter in it and fry the celeriac gently until fairly tender, just stirring and turning the vegetable for 2–3 minutes. Then increase the heat a little and fry, stirring and turning the celeriac fairly frequently, for 2–3 minutes more until the vegetable is appetisingly streaked with pale gold. Remove and keep hot.

Add the apples to the frying pan, spreading them in a single layer if possible. Fry them over medium-low heat for about 5 minutes, turning them once or twice, until slightly softened, translucent and streaked with pale gold.

Remove and reserve. Fry the walnut pieces for a few minutes until they begin to brown. Quickly return the celeriac and apple to the pan. Toss with salt and pepper and serve straight away.

SERVES 6–8

PARSNIP POPOVERS

Yorkshire pudding and roast parsnips are classic accompaniments to the Sunday roast and everybody seems to love them. In this recipe I have united batter and parsnips, which simplifies matters for the cook, and I suggest the optional addition of Cheddar cheese. The inclusion of cheese is inappropriate if the popovers are to accompany roast meat, of course, but a couple of cheesy parsnip popovers make a very enjoyable light supper if served with a crisp salad on the side.

1 lb (450 g) young parsnips
bacon fat or dripping
¼ lb/scant 1 cup (125 g) plain (all-purpose) flour
a pinch of mustard powder
2 eggs
¼ pint/⅔ cup (150 ml) each milk and water
a dash of Worcestershire sauce
Farmhouse Cheddar cheese

If using young parsnips you will simply need to scrub them and cut them into chunks. If using older parsnips it would be as well to buy a larger quantity than specified, to peel them and to cut out and discard any woody cores.

Blanch the chunks of parsnip by dropping them into a pan of fast-boiling water and bringing quickly back to the boil. Remove from the heat immediately, drain and pat dry.

Melt a little fat in a roasting tin on top of the stove. When sizzling, add the parsnip pieces and turn them to coat all over with a little fat. Transfer the tin to an oven heated to 425°F (220°C), mark 7 and cook for just 20 minutes.

Towards the end of this time grease 8 Yorkshire pudding tins or similar patty tins about 4 inches (10 cm) in diameter and thoroughly heat them in the oven.

Sift the flour, mustard powder and some salt into a mixing bowl and make a well in the centre. Break the eggs into the well and add the milk, water and a dash of Worcestershire sauce. Whisk the liquids together, then gradually blend them into the dry ingredients to make a very smooth thick creamy batter. Next cut 8 × 1 inch (2.5 cm) cubes of Cheddar cheese (optional).

Divide the parsnip pieces between the hot patty tins, pour the batter round them and, if using cheese, top each with a lump of Cheddar. Bake for about 35 minutes until the batter is puffed up and crisp and the cheese has become a molten golden pool.

SERVES 4–8

SALSIFY OR SCORZONERA FRITTERS

Salsify and its black-skinned cousin scorzonera are well worth growing. They are expensive to buy at the greengrocer's and both make very fine eating—succulent and subtle tasting. This is a good recipe for making a smallish quantity of the roots serves 6–8 people very splendidly indeed.

1½ lb (700 g) salsify or scorzonera
lemon juice and olive oil
¼ lb/scant 1 cup (125 g) well seasoned plain (all-purpose)
   flour
2 egg whites, whisked
lemon wedges, and well chilled creamy yoghurt
   flavoured with a good shake of anchovy essence

Choose roots that are long, of even thickness, with no damage to the skins and with a little bit of stalk still attached. Scrub the roots but do not trim or peel them. Choose a pan large enough to take the full length of the roots—a large non-stick frying pan with a lid is more likely to be suitable than a saucepan.

Half-fill the pan with boiling salted water. Add the roots and cook until *just* tender (bear in mind that they will be cooked again in the fritter batter). How long the roots need to be boiled depends to some extent on their thickness. I find that thick roots tend to be more tender, needing about 10 minutes; thin ones may need 15 or occasionally 20 minutes, but the only way to be certain is to watch them and to cut one open and taste it.

As soon as the roots are ready, plunge them into cold water to arrest cooking. Peel and cut the roots into 8–10 cm (3–4 inch) lengths and place them immediately in a lemon dressing—made by shaking together one part lemon juice to two parts olive oil in a screw-top jar. Set aside until completely cold, or better still for several hours.

To make the batter, beat 2 tbsp olive oil and ¼ pint/⅔ cup (150 ml) cold water into the flour, then fold in the whisked egg whites.

Drain the vegetables from the marinade, dip in batter and deep-fry in small batches at 360–375°F (185–190°C) until golden and crisp, about 2 minutes. Drain well and serve immediately with lemon wedges and yoghurt. It's the contrast of cold creamy yoghurt and piping hot crisp vegetables that makes a dish like this so irresistible.

SIMMERED ARTICHOKES

This delicately flavoured gratin is one of those useful dishes that looks after itself once popped into the oven. What is more it can be kept hot for some while without spoiling. Use semi-skimmed or whole milk as you wish. Leftovers, should there be any, can be puréed with extra milk or stock to make a fine soup. Anyone thinking of growing Jerusalem artichokes should look out for a variety called Fuseau: its tubers are larger and smoother than most.

¾ lb (350 g) trimmed weight Jerusalem artichokes
butter and a little plain (all-purpose) flour
¾ pint/scant 2 cups (425 ml) milk
freshly grated nutmeg (optional)
a small bunch of parsley
freshly grated Gruyère or Parmesan cheese (optional)

First make a thin white sauce, using 1½ tbsp each butter and flour and the milk. Season generously with salt and pepper, plus a little nutmeg if you like. Cover and set aside.

In order to obtain the required quantity of neatly sliced artichoke flesh you may need to start with 1½ lb (700 g) Jerusalem artichokes. Scrub them; I do not peel them. Cut away and discard any tiny lumps or stringy whiskers. Slice the artichokes thinly—a mandolin or food processor is quickest and gives beautifully even results. Save any odd-shaped pieces to make a soup.

Lay the slices in a generously buttered gratin dish. Arrange them, slightly overlapping like tiles; spoon some of the hot white sauce between layers, also some chopped parsley. Work quickly because artichokes discolour when they are exposed to the air. End with a good layer of the white sauce and dot with thin wafers of butter.

Bake for approximately 1½ hours at 325°F (160°C), mark 3. Exactly how long the artichokes will take depends on the thickness of the slices, the material of the dish and the idiosyncrasies of the oven: the artichokes are ready when they have absorbed most of the liquid, are tender and topped with a pale golden appetising crust.

If you want to give the gratin a rich-tasting golden finish, sprinkle the cheese over the surface and flash the dish under the grill (broiler) immediately before serving.

SERVES 4–6

COOK'S NOTEBOOK

Now that supermarket shelves are permanently groaning with plenty, there is no real reason to stow away enough provisions to see us safely through the winter. Similarly, since central heating is commonplace, a roaring log fire could be rated as a luxury rather than a necessity. But, in the country at least, the first frosts always seem to trigger some ancestral fear of the long dark nights of winters past. Folk memory is more potent than modern-day fact. As the season of mists and mellow fruitfulness draws to a close, I feel a sense of foreboding and my squirrelling instincts come to the fore.

Being a Scot I love perhaps more than most the idea of harvesting foods for free, but frugal and resourceful country cooks everywhere have always taken sensible advantage of foods growing in the wild to eke out hard-won, conventionally cultivated crops. Everyone I have talked to seems to agree that there is a special urgency about gathering in these last offerings of the year.

I like to make glowing fruit jellies, fiery sloe gin and soothing rosehip syrup. Liquid sunshine thus captured and preserved is of course energising sustenance with which to combat cold weather; but there's more to it than that. Laying in stores such as these seems like some kind of talisman—as though such vivid reminders of times of plenty will help keep alive the hope and the promise that sap-rising spring will return. This may sound fanciful now that winter is no longer the truly fearful and uncertain season it once was, but age-old superstitions can haunt

us still. At any rate, I have found that tiptoeing into the larder just to look at the goodies in store has a curiously calming and comforting effect, alleviating the worst of winter blues.

Prunes, often despised because of their sad institutional image, are particular favourites of mine. Plumped in port with a dash of orange zest and tea, they make a magnificent compôte. Mixed with good sausagemeat and chestnuts they make a fine stuffing for turkey or chicken. Wrapped in rashers of fat streaky bacon they make an admirable savoury. Best of all perhaps are *Spiced Prunes*, which are wonderful for enlivening winter casseroles and pies made with rabbit, and excellent served with coarse country pâtés and other cold meats.

Put 2 lb (900 g) stoned prunes into a large bowl together with a generous 1¼ pints/3 cups (750 ml) cider vinegar, 1¼ lb/3⅓ cups (575 g) soft dark-brown sugar. Add the thinly pared rind of 2 oranges, 2 cinnamon sticks and 2 tbsp crushed coriander seeds, all tied up in buttermuslin, and leave to soak overnight. Turn the contents of the bowl into a pan, bring very slowly to simmering point, cover and simmer for 8 minutes. Transfer the prunes to clean warm jars and boil the syrup until reduced to 1 pint/ 2½ cups (575 ml) before pouring it over the prunes to cover them completely.

The Sunday before Advent, or "Stir Up Sunday" as it is still called in some areas, is by tradition the last day on which to make Christmas pudding, although most people agree that the sooner the pudding is made the better it tastes. The other

important thing is to stir the pudding mixture very thoroughly indeed. This would be an arm-aching business if left to the cook alone. But it isn't. Thanks to the ruse introduced by some ingenious woman many years ago, the cook's lone labour has been transformed into a pleasurable family ritual as everyone queues to take his or her turn at stirring the pudding in order to make a wish. The fun and excitement of it all is such that our family has created its own new "tradition": now everyone joins in stirring the mincemeat as well as the pudding and so has the chance to make a second wish.

By the time the pudding, mincemeat and other sweetmeats have been made I feel almost ready to face any rigours winter may hold, but I don't feel entirely safe until I have stocked up with such things as nightlights, candles and a couple of gas cylinders for my little camping gas cooker. Theoretically these are emergency stores, a precaution against possible power cuts, but in practice the candles and nightlights are pure self-indulgence. I have a passion for them and try to keep them alight, like the yule log burning in the grate constantly through the 12 days of Christmas. Our pagan forefathers thought such things necessary to ward off evil spirits associated with the dark, and Christians perpetuated the practice "to lighten our spiritual darkness". I only know these are the shortest and darkest days of the year, the time when the need to be surrounded by comforting things is greatest, and candle-light certainly fills the house with a softness and warmth that brash electricity cannot match.

Pies and Puddings

Napoleon called us a nation of shopkeepers. He might equally well have called us a nation of pastry cooks, for no other country can match our splendid and varied repertoire of puddings and pies.

Every region of Britain boasts its own specialities: think of bridies, badgers and bolsters; of clangers, coffyns and clooties; of oggies, pluggas and duffs. Many are admirably frugal, ekeing out tiny scraps of meat with plenty of vegetable and pastry padding. And many are ingeniously shaped self-contained lunch boxes, solidly made for safe carrying in the saddle-bag of a rider or in the pocket of a miner or farmer. Delicious and ever popular though these humble everyday offerings are, the puddings and pies we love best (and those that win accolades from other nations) are the rich and luxurious versions traditionally reserved for festive occasions and for entertaining in style.

Here's a reminder of the quantities and methods used for five favourite pastry recipes.

SHORTCRUST PASTRY

¾ lb/scant 2½ cups (340 g) plain (all-purpose) white flour, or ¾ lb/scant 2½ cups (340 g) self-raising wholemeal (whole wheat) flour, or 6 oz/generous 1 cup (175 g) each plain white and plain wholemeal flour; 3 oz/¾ stick (85 g) butter or margarine; 3 oz/scant ½ cup (85 g) lard or white vegetable fat; about 4 tbsp cold water.

Sift the flour(s), adding a pinch of salt if wished. Cut, then rub in fat. Stir in cold water to bind. Draw the dough into a ball and knead lightly.

CRISP CHEESE PASTRY

6 oz/1½ sticks (175 g) butter or margarine; 5 oz/1¼ cups (140 g) grated mature Cheddar cheese; ¾ lb/scant 2½ cups (350 g) self-raising flour; ½ tsp each salt and mustard powder; a large pinch of cayenne pepper; 6 tbsp cold water.

Put the butter or margarine into a freezer for an hour to make it icy cold and hard. Sift the flour, salt, mustard powder and cayenne. Grate the thoroughly chilled butter or margarine on to the dry ingredients and mix lightly. Stir in the cheese and mix to a firm dough with the cold water.

SUETCRUST PASTRY

¾ lb/scant 2½ cups (350 g) self-raising flour; 1 tsp baking powder; 1 tsp salt (or sugar for sweet dishes); 1 tsp dried thyme (or allspice for sweet dishes); 6 oz/1½ cups (175 g) grated or shredded suet; about 6 fl oz/¾ cup (175 ml) cold water.

Sift the flour and baking powder. Stir in the flavourings and suet, then enough cold water to make a soft dough. Roll the dough into a ball and knead very lightly.

HOT-WATER CRUST PASTRY

1 tsp each salt and freshly ground black pepper; 1 lb/generous 3 cups (450 g) plain (all-purpose) flour; 3 oz/scant ½ cup (75 g) lard; 1 oz/¼ stick (25 g) butter or dripping; 8 fl oz/1 cup (225 ml) water.

Stir the salt and pepper into the sifted flour. Bring the fats and water to the boil. Pour the mixture on to the flour and stir briskly until the dough forms a ball. Knead lightly then cover the dough with an upturned bowl and leave for 15 minutes.

PUFF PASTRY

1 lb/generous 3 cups (450 g) strong plain (all-purpose) flour; 1 lb/4 sticks (450 g) butter; 2 tsp lemon juice; 9½ fl oz/scant 1¼ cups (285 ml) cold water.

Sift the flour, adding a pinch of salt if wished. Cut, then rub one quarter of the butter into the flour. Bind the dough with the lemon juice and water. Knead and chill for 20 minutes.

Dust the remaining butter with flour and roll it out to an oblong about ½ inch (1 cm) thick. Roll the chilled dough to an oblong about ½ inch (1 cm) wider than the slab of butter and slightly more than three times as long. Lay the butter in the centre of the pastry. Fold the bottom third of pastry up over the butter, and the top third down. Seal the open pastry edges by pressing with the rolling pin.

Give the pastry a quarter turn to bring the sealed edges to the top and bottom. Press the dough gently with the rolling pin, four or five times from centre to top, then four or five times from centre to bottom, to distribute the air. Quickly and lightly roll out the dough to an oblong three times as long as it is wide. Fold the bottom third of the pastry up, and the top third down, keeping the edges straight. Seal the open edges. Wrap and chill for 30 minutes.

Return the chilled pastry to the work surface, positioning it so that the sealed edges are at top and bottom, and repeat the rolling, folding, sealing and chilling sequence five times. Puff pastry is best made a day before using. It will keep in the refrigerator for 2–3 days.

WILTSHIRE PLAIT (PAGE 116)

WILTSHIRE PLAIT

Surprise nuggets of melting cheese and bites of Bramley nestling in the pork make this a very popular pie with my family and friends. Good news for the cook: despite its handsome appearance, Wiltshire Plait is cheap, quick, easy to make, and excellent both hot and cold.

10 oz (275 g) lean end belly of pork (salt pork), boneless and de-rinded weight
half a small cooking apple
2 oz (50 g) mature Cheddar cheese
1 very small onion
1 garlic clove
4–5 tbsp fresh chopped parsley
salt and freshly ground black pepper
1 egg
puff pastry made with 6 oz/generous 1 cup (175 g) flour (page 114) or ¾ lb (350 g) ready-made puff pastry

Mince the pork. Cut the apple and cheese into small dice. Chop the onion very finely indeed, and crush the garlic. Mix these ingredients together with the chopped parsley and plenty of salt and pepper. Bind the mixture with half the beaten egg.

Roll out the pastry to a 10 inch (25 cm) square. Pat the pork mixture into a fat sausage shape and lay it down the centre of the pastry. Cut the pastry diagonally into ½ inch (1 cm) strips on either side of the pork mixture. Damp the end of each pastry strip, then fold the strips, alternately from each side, over the meat filling to create a lattice or plait (braid) effect. Seal the pastry ends and glaze over with the remaining beaten egg to brown the crust.

Slide the plait on to a damp baking tray and bake at 425°F (220°C), mark 7 for 20 minutes, then at 350°F (180°C), mark 4 for a further 20–25 minutes.
SERVES 4

RAISED GAME PIE

It is always reassuring to have a handsome cut-and-come-again pie in the larder, and I find this an invaluable recipe for the festive season. Making such a pie takes considerable time and effort so it makes sense to make a large pie while you're at it. Pheasant, partridge, grouse, pigeon, guinea fowl, chicken and turkey are all suitable ingredients.

2 lb (900 g) feathered game or poultry meat, boned and skinned weight
salt, pepper and ground allspice
6 tbsp brandy
2 pig's trotters
¾ lb/6 cups (350 g) mushrooms
a little butter or oil
1 lb (450 g) green streaky bacon, de-rinded
¾ lb (350 g) pie veal
a bunch parsley
1 small onion
hot-water crust pastry made with 1 lb/generous 3 cups (450 g) flour (page 114)
beaten egg to glaze

Cut the raw game or poultry into slivers and put it into a bowl. Sprinkle generously with salt, pepper and allspice. Pour on the brandy, cover and leave in a cool place. Use the carcasses of the birds and the pig's trotters to make a good stock. De-grease and reduce it to just over ½ pint/1¼ cups (300 ml); it should be very savoury in flavour and should set to a firm jelly when cold. If pig's trotters are unavailable, set the stock with 2 tsp gelatine powder.

Chop the livers of the birds and sauté them

together with the sliced mushrooms in a little hot fat or oil. Set aside to cool. Mince the bacon together with the veal. Season lavishly with salt, pepper and allspice, then stir in plenty of chopped fresh parsley and the very finely chopped onion.

Make the pastry, cover it with an upturned bowl and leave for 15 minutes so that the dough becomes pleasantly malleable—if it is too hot it will slide down the pie tin; if too cold it will be difficult to mould.

Lightly grease a large traditional hinged and fluted pie tin or a 8 in (20 cm) round cake tin with a removable base. Leaving a generous quarter of the dough to keep warm under the upturned bowl, put the rest into the pie tin.

Use your hands to shape the dough over the base, then work it gradually and evenly up the sides of the mould and extend it nearly ½ inch (1 cm) above the top of the tin. Put the filling into the pastry-lined tin, layering or mixing the ingredients as you wish. Pack the filling quite firmly against the base and sides of the crust to keep the pie in good shape, and mound the top nicely in the centre.

Roll out the remaining pastry to make a lid. Damp the edges, position the lid and seal it firmly against the pie walls. Make a large steam hole in the centre of the lid and hold it open by half-inserting a piece of rolled card. Decorate and glaze the pie with the beaten egg. Stand the pie tin on a baking tray and bake at 425°F (220°C), mark 7 for 20 minutes, then at 350°F (180°C), mark 4 for 1¾ hours. Re-glaze the pie occasionally as it cooks, or cover with brown paper if it is browning too fast.

Remove the pie from the oven and let it stand for 40 minutes before carefully and gently easing the sides of the mould away from the pie. Glaze the sides of the pie and return the pie to the oven for 10 minutes or so to colour the pastry sides.

Let the cooked pie stand for about 15 minutes before pouring into it enough stock to fill any gaps created by the meats shrinking during cooking. The stock should be barely warm and it should be added slowly to avoid flooding—I advise the use of a jam funnel and a spoon. Store the pie in a cold larder for 24–36 hours before eating. Do not wrap or cover the pie until it is completely cold or the pastry will lose its delicious crispness.

SERVES 14

BEEF WELLINGTON

Of all pies this must be the most lavish and extravagant—deliberately so, I imagine, since the recipe was presumably created for and first served at a grand banquet held to celebrate the Iron Duke's victory over Napoleon.

2 lb (900 g) well-hung fillet of beef
1 small garlic clove
salt and freshly ground black pepper
2 tsp brandy
1 oz/¼ stick (25 g) clarified butter
¼ lb/2 cups (125 g) mushrooms
1 small onion
puff pastry made with ½ lb/generous 1½ cups (225 g)
    flour (page 114) or 1 lb (450 g) ready-made puff pastry
2 oz (50 g) smooth-textured pâté
1 beaten egg, to glaze

Trim all fat and membrane from the beef. Rub the flesh with the cut garlic clove, then with a good grinding of pepper. Brush the meat with the brandy and tie it into a neat bolster shape with string.

Thoroughly heat a heavy-based frying pan. Add the butter and, when the butter foam dies down, add the beef. Brown and seal it all over. Then reduce heat and fry the beef more gently for another 10 minutes, turning the joint as necessary to encourage even cooking. Remove the beef from the pan and allow it to become completely cold.

Chop the mushrooms and onions quite finely. Soften them in the fat remaining in the pan. Drain well, season and allow to become cold.

Roll out the pastry to an oblong a little wider than the fillet of beef and more than twice its length. Remove the string from the beef and lay the joint down one end of the pastry. Spread the pâté over the meat and lay the vegetables on top.

Brush the pastry edges with beaten egg. Fold the long end of pastry over the meat and seal all round to make a secure parcel. Decorate with trimmings, glaze and make steam slits.

Slide the parcel on to a damp baking sheet and bake it for 20 minutes at 425°F (220°C), mark 7. Reduce oven temperature to 350°F (180°C), mark 4 and bake for a further 10–15 minutes or so depending on how rare or well cooked you wish the beef to be.

SERVES 6

RAISED GAME PIE (PAGE 116)

LITTLE LEMON AND HERB CHICKEN PIES

Creamy and delicately flavoured, these are unusually luxurious individual chicken pies. You can of course use one large pie dish if you prefer, and turkey can be used in place of chicken.

8 spring onions (scallions)
2 oz/1 cup (50 g) fresh chopped parsley
2 tsp dried lemon thyme
2 lemons
6 boneless portions of chicken breast
½ oz/1 tbsp (15 g) butter
2 tbsp plain (all-purpose) flour
8 fl oz/1 cup (225 ml) chicken stock
½ pint/1¼ cups (275 ml) double (heavy) or whipping cream
shortcrust pastry made with ¾ lb/scant 2½ cups (340 g) flour (page 114), preferably half white, half wholemeal (whole wheat) flour
1 beaten egg, to glaze

Chop the spring onions finely, green parts as well as white. Mix them with the parsley, the lemon thyme and the finely grated zest of both lemons. Set the mixture aside.

Cut the chicken into large bite-size pieces. Colour them lightly in the butter and reserve. Stir the flour into the fat remaining in the frying pan, then blend in the stock and cream and bring the sauce to simmering point, stirring all the time. Add the prepared herb mixture, a good squeeze of lemon juice, some pepper and a little salt. Push the herbs well down into the sauce and bring back to simmering point.

Away from the heat, stir the chicken into the sauce. Let the mixture cool a little while you prepare the pastry.

Divide the pastry into six pieces. Roll out each piece until it is a bit larger than the top of an individual pie dish. Cut strips from the outer edges of the pastry and press them on to the wetted rims of the pie dishes. Divide the filling between the pie dishes. Dampen the pastry rims, cover with the pastry lids and seal well. Decorate, glaze with beaten egg and make steam slits.

Slide the pie dishes on to baking trays. Bake for 20 minutes at 400°F (200°C), mark 6, and for 20 minutes at 350°F (180°C), mark 4. Then switch off the heat but leave the pies in the oven for a further 15–20 minutes. The reason for this is that the delicate flavour of the pies is best when they are not too hot.

SERVES 6

RUNAWAY PIE

Although best made with hare, this transforms rabbit into a celebratory dish.

1 hare or rabbit (preferably wild), jointed
½ tsp dried rosemary
a very generous pinch ground cloves
1 lb (450 g) belly of pork (salt pork), boned weight
¾ lb (350 g) onions
2 crushed garlic cloves
4 fl oz/½ cup (125 ml) Marsala
½ pint/1¼ cups (275 ml) dry cider
the finely grated zest of an orange
1½ tbsp each softened butter and plain (all-purpose) flour
1 dozen spiced prunes (see page 113)
puff pastry made with ½ lb/generous 1½ cups (225 g) flour (page 114), or 1 lb (450 g) ready-made puff pastry

Soak the hare or rabbit joints in cold salted water for 1½ hours. Drain, cover with fresh cold water, bring to the boil and simmer for 3 minutes. Drain and dry well. (This soaking and blanching can be omitted if using hutch rabbit.)

Pound the rosemary with a mortar and pestle to soften its spikiness. Add the ground cloves and plenty of salt and pepper, and use the mixture to dust the joints. Seal the joints in a little hot fat in a frying pan, then transfer them to a flameproof casserole. Cube the pork and chop the onions into large chunks. Colour both ingredients in the fat remaining in the pan and transfer them to the casserole.

Put the Marsala into the pan and stir to scrape meaty sediment from the pan base. Add the cider, bring to the boil and pour into the casserole. Add garlic and orange zest. Cover and cook at 325°F (160°C), mark 3 for about 1½ hours.

Transfer the meats and vegetables to a large pie dish. Bring the gravy to the boil. Add the butter and flour mixture, a small nugget at a time, and cook, stirring continuously, until the sauce is smooth and slightly thickened. Adjust seasoning to taste. Pour into the pie dish, cover and store in a cold larder overnight.

Add the spiced prunes to the pie dish. Roll out the pastry until it is slightly larger than the top of the pie dish. Cut a strip from the outer edge of the pastry and press it on to the wetted rim of the pie dish. Wet the pastry rim, cover with the pastry lid and seal well. Decorate, glaze with beaten egg and make steam slits.

Slide the pie dish on to a baking tray. Bake for 25 minutes at 425°F (220°C), mark 7, then for 15 minutes at 350°F (180°C), mark 4.

SERVES 6

COOK'S NOTEBOOK

The problem of filling the hungry gap between the end of summer and the arrival of Christmas is nothing new, and country cooks are traditionally adept at coping. They are instinctively canny, resourceful and frugal. It goes against the grain to add any ingredient to the cooking pot unless it makes a positive contribution. There is also distaste for the idea of discarding anything when some vestige of usefulness can still be wrung from it. For example, the outer leaves of the cabbage are sensibly thought too tough to warrant being lightly steamed and served as a vegetable. They are saved instead for "wrappers", used to parcel up other foods for the long and gentle braising which renders them tender.

The archetypal symbol of this "waste not want not" approach is the stockpot, in which seemingly naked meat bones are simmered for hours to extract every last drop of their flavour and goodness. Cynics regard this exercise as Scrooge-like, or playing at being self-sufficient, or both; they are quick to point out that it is much cheaper to buy stock cubes than to make your own. Their economics may be sound, but I belong to the school that favours stock-making.

Now that the freezer has largely replaced the breadbin, staling bread is no longer the problem it was. This would suggest that many of our traditional recipes are in danger of being lost. But country cooks will surely continue to use them, occasionally at least. There is of course no virtue in old for the sake of old—that is as pointless as *nouvelle* for the sake of new—

but it seems frankly foolish to abandon, out-of-hand, recipes that have established themselves as tried and true favourites down the years. In fact many of our traditional bread-based recipes seem particularly suitable for serving during those lean and hungry weeks leading up to Christmas. These recipes are not only cheap and easy to cook, they are also deliciously warming and filling.

Think of dishes like *Apple Charlotte*, with its stiff purée of tart fruit and its deliciously contrasting slices of bread, buttered so they "fry" to a crackle of gold during baking. Think of *Poor Knights of Windsor*—lucky knights to be feasted in such a way. Think of *Bread and Butter Pudding*, studded with muscatel raisins and freckled with cinnamon, a nursery dish which has recently won the Foodies' seal of approval. Few can resist *Thunder and Lightning*, one of the quickest, easiest and most wicked of all puddings: a slice of bread fried in butter or rosemary-flavoured lard, served piping hot with a drizzle of golden syrup spooned over and a dollop of chilled clotted cream.

Bread most often appears in savoury recipes in the form of breadcrumbs. Careful cooks have frequently used crumbs, softened and swollen with milk or water, as an alternative to flour for thickening soups and sauces. They have also made a habit of mixing crumbs with onions and herbs or other flavourings to make expensive meats and fish go further. Indeed some of the dishes we regard as Great British Classics probably originated as economy measures. *Bread Sauce*,

Sage and Onion Stuffing and *Lemon and Parsley Forcemeat Balls* are just three well-known examples.

The inclusion of breadcrumbs in our minced-meat dishes is peculiarly British. Whereas Continental sausages and pâtés tend to be pure meat, British bangers and meatloaves nearly always include breadcrumbs. Glamorgan Sausages take matters to the extreme: made from breadcrumbs, cheese, eggs, onion or leek, and herbs, these "sausages" contain no meat at all.

Fairly fresh breadcrumbs can be used to replace up to half of the flour usually used in suet puddings, dumplings and savoury crumbles—the results are appetisingly light.

Breadcrumbs are sensationally good at protecting other foods in cooking. Delicate ingredients such as white fish fillets, tender chicken breasts, veal and liver are all easily scorched and spoiled when subjected to the fierce heat of frying or grilling. So are dishes such as homemade fishcakes, rissoles and croquettes—which are, of course, some of the frugal cook's favourite ways of using up small quantities of leftovers. Egging-and-breadcrumbing provides just the protection needed, and produces that contrast of crisp coating and succulent food sealed within that everyone seems to love. What is more, egging-and-crumbing makes foods a little more nutritious and filling without greatly adding to their cost. These foods are traditionally fried but, as health-conscious cooks have discovered, if brushed with just a whisper of oil they can be grilled. Just as delicious and healthier.

STEAK, KIDNEY AND OYSTER PUDDING

I find it best to part-cook this most famous of meat puddings a day ahead of serving. This gives you the chance to check the gravy for seasoning and consistency, and it makes for a shortish steaming time—which produces a particularly light and delicious pastry.

generous 1½ lb (750 g) chuck steak
¾ lb (scant 350 g) ox kidney
1½ oz/scant ¼ cup (40 g) beef dripping
2 onions
2 tbsp plain (all-purpose) flour
2 tsp lemon juice
1 tsp Worcestershire sauce
¾ pint/scant 2 cups (425 ml) beef stock
1 tsp dried thyme
crushed parsley stalks tied with string
salt and freshly ground black pepper
suetcrust pastry made with ¾ lb/scant 2½ cups (350 g)
   flour (page 114)
18–24 fine fresh oysters

Cut the steak into large cubes, dice the kidney and chop the onions. Briskly sear and seal the meats, in batches, in a little very hot dripping, and transfer them to a casserole. Add the remaining fat to the pan and fry the onions briefly. Sprinkle on the flour and stir it in. Pour on the liquids and bring to the boil, stirring. Add the herbs and a good seasoning of salt and pepper.

Pour the gravy over the meats, cover the casserole and cook at 300°F (150°C), mark 2 for 1½ hours.

Remove the bundle of parsley stalks and check the gravy for seasoning. Cover the casserole again and store it in a cold larder for a few hours, or preferably overnight.

Make the pastry and use about three-quarters of it to line a large, well-buttered pudding basin. Put the cold meat mixture into the basin. Fold surplus pastry lining over the filling and damp the pastry edges.

Make a lid from the remaining pastry and press the edges to seal well. Cover with buttered and pleated foil and tie securely under the basin rim.

Steam for 1½–2 hours, topping up the pan with extra boiling water if necessary.

When the pudding is cooked, remove wrappings, dry the basin and tie a crisp white linen napkin round it.

Cut a slice from the suetcrust and add the raw oysters and their liquor to the filling immediately before serving.

SERVES 6–8

STEAK, KIDNEY AND OYSTER PUDDING

VENISON AND CRANBERRY PUDDING

Like Steak, Kidney and Oyster Pudding, this is a splendid dish for cold-weather eating, and it never fails to delight and impress overseas visitors. When fresh cranberries are unavailable I use frozen red-currants instead. Thaw but do not cook them: stir them into the pudding when the crust is cut open for serving.

2–2½ lb (900 g–1.1 kg) stewing venison
½ lb/4 cups (225 g) mushrooms
1 large onion
a little butter and oil
2 tbsp plain (all-purpose) flour
¼ pint/⅔ cup (150 ml) red wine
12 fl oz/1½ cups (350 ml) stock
2–3 tbsp redcurrant jelly
1 tsp finely grated orange zest
2 tsp Dijon mustard
suetcrust pastry made with ¾ lb/scant 2½ cups (350 g) flour (page 114) and flavoured with 1 tsp each dried thyme and grated orange zest
½ lb/2 cups (225 g) fresh cranberries

Cut the venison into large cubes, slice the mushrooms thickly and chop the onion. Sauté the mushrooms in a little very hot fat, driving off most of their moisture to concentrate the flavour. Remove from the pan and reserve.

Briskly sear and seal the venison, in batches, and transfer it to a casserole. Add more fat to the pan and, when very hot, fry the onion briefly. Sprinkle on the flour and stir it in. Pour on the wine and stock and bring to the boil, stirring. Add the jelly, orange zest and mustard and a good seasoning of salt and pepper.

Pour the gravy into the casserole, cover and cook at 300°F (150°C), mark 2 for about 1½ hours. Adjust seasoning to taste, cover the casserole again and store it in a cold larder overnight.

Make the pastry and use about three-quarters of it to line a large, well-buttered pudding basin. Stir the raw, fresh cranberries into the cold venison mixture and add the reserved mushrooms. Put this filling into the pastry-lined basin. Fold surplus pastry lining over the filling and damp the pastry edges. Cover with a lid made from the remaining pastry and press to seal well. Cover with buttered and pleated foil and tie securely under the basin rim. Steam for 1½–2 hours, topping up the water if necessary.

SERVES 6–8

PIGEON PUFF

The bonus of this recipe is that it not only makes a sumptuous pie but produces plenty of rich game stock which can be used as the basis for nourishing soups in the following days. Olives which are sold loose or packed in brine tend to taste a little bitter. For a sweeter, more olivey flavour, drop the olives into a pan of cold water, bring to the boil and simmer for 5 minutes. Drain, then cool under cold running water and dry before using in cooking.

6 pigeons
6 oz/3 cups (175 g) button mushrooms
a little butter and oil
18 shallots
1 thickish gammon rasher (ham slice), cubed
fresh thyme
fresh parsley
2 generous tbsp plain (all-purpose) flour
12½ fl oz/generous 1½ cups (365 ml) pigeon stock
2 tbsp brandy
2 tsp tomato purée
2 garlic cloves
puff pastry made with 10 oz/2 cups (275 g) flour (page 114), or 1¼ lb (550 g) ready-made puff pastry
1 beaten egg, to glaze
18 black (ripe) olives

Cut the breast meat from the birds and reserve. Use the carcasses to make a richly flavoured game stock—a little of which is needed for this recipe; the rest can be saved, together with pigeon meat picked from the bones, to use for soup.

Sauté the mushrooms in a little very hot butter and oil; remove and reserve. Lightly colour the pigeon breast meat and transfer it to a flameproof casserole. Barely colour the shallots and gammon in the oil and arrange them on top of the pigeon meat. Add several sprigs of thyme and a bundle of lightly crushed parsley stalks, neatly tied together with string.

Melt a little more butter in the frying pan. Blend in the flour, then the stock, brandy and tomato purée, and cook, stirring continuously, until the sauce reaches boiling point. Season with salt and pepper according to taste and add the crushed garlic.

Pour the sauce into the casserole and cover with a well-fitting lid. Cook at 300–325°F (150–160°C), mark 2–3 until the pigeon is tender, approximately 1¼ hours.

Fish out the bundle of herbs, squeezing them between a pair of spoons so that all the flavoursome juices drip back into the casserole. Set the casserole aside in a cold place or larder overnight.

To make the giant, lidless vol-au-vent case in which to serve the pigeon, first roll out the puff pastry and cut from it a 10 inch (25.5 cm) circle using a dinner plate or saucepan lid as a template.

Then, using an 8 inch (20.5 cm) template, cut out the centre of the large pastry circle. Re-roll the small pastry circle to make a 10 inch (25.5 cm) round. Place this on a baking sheet, brush the edges with beaten egg, and position the pastry band on top of it.

Prick the pastry base and brush the pastry band with beaten egg. Use any left-over scraps of pastry to make decorative fleurons; glaze them and add to the baking sheet. Sprinkle the baking sheet with cold water and bake at 425°F (220°C), mark 7 for about 30 minutes until the pastry is puffed up and golden.

Lift the pigeon meat out of the casserole. Slice it thickly and return it to the casserole. Add the reserved mushrooms and the stoned black olives. Cover the mixture, place over a low heat and reheat gently but thoroughly while the pastry is cooking.

Stir a good quantity of chopped fresh parsley into the hot pigeon mixture, pile the filling carefully into the puffed-up pastry case and serve straight away.

SERVES 6

SIX O'CLOCK PARCELS

Savoury mouthfuls like these are just the thing to cheer carol singers on their way, to nibble before a circus or pantomime outing, or to serve with leisurely pre-dinner drinks in front of a roaring log fire.

crisp cheese pastry with ¾ lb/scant 2½ cups (350 g) flour (page 114)
½ lb/4 cups (225 g) mushrooms
1 small onion
a little butter
2 tbsp dry sherry
1 oz/¼ cup (25 g) coarsely chopped walnuts
6 oz (175 g) smooth-textured chicken liver pâté
1 beaten egg, to glaze
sesame seeds and paprika to garnish

Make the pastry, wrap and chill it while preparing the filling.

Chop the mushrooms and onion very finely. Melt a knob of butter in a small pan and fry the onion gently until transparent. Stir in the mushrooms and sherry and cook for 3–4 minutes. Remove from the heat, stir in the walnuts, a good seasoning of pepper and a little salt. Let the mixture cool a little before thoroughly blending the chicken liver pâté into it.

Roll the pastry as thinly as possible and cut out about 24 circles, using a 3½ inch (9 cm) plain, round cutter.

Place a heaped teaspoonful of the chicken liver mixture on one side of each pastry circle and brush the pastry edges with beaten egg. Fold over and seal each parcel firmly. Glaze and sprinkle with a few sesame seeds.

Slide the parcels on to baking sheets and bake at 425°F (220°C), mark 7 for 12 minutes or so until golden brown. These are best served warm rather than piping hot from the oven, dusted with a little paprika.

MAKES ABOUT 24

Festive Birds

Turkey has held pride of place on the Christmas dinner table for many years now and I can't help feeling that the time has come for a change. For one thing, turkey no longer seems quite the treat that it was. In the old days, Christmas was the only occasion on which turkey was served, so we looked forward to it with something akin to the greedy excitement of children awaiting their Christmas stockings.

Now turkey is available all year round and its reputation for being one of the leanest and healthiest of meats means that we eat it with increasing frequency throughout the year. So it hardly seems an inspired choice for a special celebratory occasion, particularly considering all the other birds there are to choose from—feathered game and domesticated fowl in deliciously tempting variety.

Some of the options are given here. Which will suit you best depends on several factors, including the numbers to be catered for, and whether you like the idea of finishing the bird at one sitting or want it to see you through the whole of the Christmas festivities.

If big is your idea of beautiful, goose is the only real alternative to turkey, but there is a wide choice of smaller birds too. Indeed some birds deserving consideration are small enough to warrant one per person, which saves the carver considerable time and trouble, is fun for the diners and ensures the food is piping hot when served. These are points worth bearing in mind when planning winter dinner parties as well as the Christmas Day menu.

GOOSE

This ought to be the number-one choice for traditionalists, as its associations with Christmas go back down the ages—turkey is, in truth, a relatively modern upstart. The only trouble with goose is that many people seem to have an in-built prejudice against it. I confess I refused to cook or eat it for years. Then I test-cooked a whole gaggle and discovered just how beautifully flavoured, succulent and rich goose can be, "like superior duck" as one of my family put it. If you have never eaten goose, I recommend it. If you have had a bad experience of it I urge you to try it again.

Apart from choosing a top-quality fresh bird, the secret of success is to cosset the goose during cooking because, although it is naturally fatty, there is a curious tendency for the breast-meat to dry out. It is also crucial not to overcook it or the flavour will be spoiled and the flesh will toughen.

The weight of an oven-ready goose is usually 9–15 lb (4–7 kg), although larger and smaller birds can be found. Bear in mind that the ratio of carcass to flesh is much higher in goose than in turkey; also that considerable weight is lost as fat exuded in cooking. So it is prudent to allow a minimum of 1 lb (450 g) oven-ready weight per serving. Also, remember that you will definitely want to have plenty of leftovers for serving at later meals; for, unlike turkey, which is frankly as dreary as sawdust third time around, succulent flavoursome goose makes superb cold eating.

DUCK

Until recently, duck was a problem for a party; the average-size bird of 4 lb (1.8 kg) was ample for 3 but caused the carver to panic when serving 4. Larger ducks are now available. Newest and best are the free-range, second-feather ducks. These are bred to 14 weeks instead of the usual 7 so the meat is more mature (by which I mean richer in flavour, not tougher) and they weigh in at up to 9 lb (4 kg). They are genuinely meaty enough to serve 6 generously. Supplies are not yet plentiful, but where second-feather duck is on sale you will note that it is simply labelled "duck"—the word "duckling" being used by the trade to describe smaller, younger birds. The practical alternative to second-feather duck is duck joints. These are easy to buy, and solve the carving problem effortlessly, enabling you to cater for precisely the number of people you want without wastage or surplus.

PHEASANT

Pheasant is the best known game bird and some would say it makes the best eating—a fine feast for 3–4 people. The hen pheasant is smaller than her mate and less showy but sweeter to eat. Like all game birds, pheasant is suitable for roasting only if young. The one "fault" of pheasant, even young pheasant, is a tendency for the breast meat to be dry. Take great care to protect it in cooking: anoint it by slipping some butter or soft cheese under the breast skin, or give it a waistcoat of bacon, or roast it breast down, or pot-roast rather than open roast it. You could even play very safe and do several of these things.

PARTRIDGE

A light hand in the kitchen is essential to do partridge proper justice: it is a bird of subtle flavour, easily spoiled if hung for too long or served with strong-tasting accompaniments. The grey-legged

FORESTER'S PHEASANT (PAGE 133)

variety is much better to eat than the red-legged sort. When 3 months old, or so, partridge weighs about 1 lb (450 g), it is tender and plump-breasted, just right for roasting. I allow 1 bird per person. This is generous but it saves the hassle of splitting partridge in half between cooking and serving, and giving each person a whole bird makes for a sense of occasion.

GUINEA-FOWL

This small domesticated bird is a decorative creature with elegant black and white (or occasionally grey and white) spotted feathers, a few of which are left unplucked to distinguish it from plebeian chicken in the butcher's shop. Considerably more expensive than chicken, it is also much more tasty than the average chicken on sale today. Its flavour could be said to be halfway house between chicken and pheasant, and this delicate gamey quality led the Victorians to think of guinea-fowl as out-of-season pheasant. It is a good choice of celebratory bird when catering for small numbers as guinea-fowl rarely weigh more than 2½ lb (1.1 kg), but take special care to protect the flesh from drying out during cooking.

POULET NOIR

Indigenous to Aquitaine, this black-legged and black-feathered breed of chicken is a newcomer here, introduced by the innovative company that was the first (and remains the only) UK producer of corn-fed chicken. *Poulet noir* is being promoted as "the gourmet's chicken", which is off-putting, but the bird itself makes excellent eating. The taste is reminiscent of guinea-fowl or the best free-range chicken. The meat is pale, lean, notably firmer than ordinary chicken and juicier, which means it is as good to eat cold as hot. Weights range from 2½ lb (1.1 kg) upwards. Use poulet noir instead of pheasant or guinea-fowl in recipes for either, or treat like chicken.

QUAIL

Although quail is shot as game in some parts of the world, those that find their way on to our tables are farmed. These very small birds are mild-tasting and there is little meat on them.

Some say that to serve less than 2 per person is starvation rations. I disagree—although this may sound at odds with my generous approach to partridge. I'm not suggesting that anyone would grow fat by eating 2 quails but I think that presenting each diner with a whole bird of their own is what really pleases. Two birds is overdoing it, I feel, particularly in the context of a party, when several courses plus cheese and fruit may be served.

Having said that, quails are of course very small

birds and the cook must take great care to prevent them looking pathetically waif-like on the plate. Fatten them up, literally, with stuffing. I also recommend crossing the quail's legs and tucking the ends through a slit in the breast. This makes the bird sit up, sergeant-major fashion—shoulders back, chest puffed out with pride so to speak—and is easier than trussing so small a bird.

Quails are stocked by some delicatessens as well as by butchers and game dealers. Often the little birds are frozen, not fresh, and although I am fundamentally prejudiced against frozen meats, I must admit I find they emerge from the icy ordeal tender and tasty. They are usually packed in fours or sixes, and are sometimes ready boned.

Quail is the antithesis of turkey. Whereas a gargantuan turkey might almost feed a family for the full 12 days of Christmas, tiny quails are guaranteed to be finished at one sitting. If you usually serve your Christmas feast in the middle of the day, your holiday rest may have been spoiled in the past by having to make a start on the turkey at the crack of dawn. Quails are so quick to cook that they could be the best Christmas present in the world.

PLUM PERFECT GOOSE

There is nothing fancy about this recipe but it makes supremely good eating—hot and cold. When roasting goose, it is usual to allow 15 minutes per 1 lb (450 g), but the larger the bird the less time it needs per pound. It is best to cook it no longer than necessary, so I advise 12–13 minutes per 1 lb (450 g) for a bird weighing 11 lb (5 kg) or over. The plum sauce keeps well for a month or more if stored in a cold larder so it can be prepared well ahead.

1 oven-ready goose weighing 11–12 lb (5–5½ kg)
1 onion and 1 orange
¾ pint/scant 2 cups (425 ml) goose-giblet stock
a generous glass of dry cider or wine
ground allspice and cinnamon
1 × 1 lb (450 g) jar damson jam
a little raspberry (page 55) or red-wine vinegar
a little sunflower or safflower oil

To make 1 lb (450 g) of plum sauce, put the contents of a 1 lb (450 g) jar of damson jam into the top part of a double-boiler. Add some raspberry or red-wine vinegar (3 tbsp vinegar for home-made jam, or 3½ tbsp for shop-bought jam), plus the zest of 1 orange and ¼ tsp ground cinnamon.

Place over barely simmering water and heat

gently, stirring occasionally, until the jam is warm and runny and blended with the vinegar. Rub through a fine sieve to make a smooth purée, then gradually beat in 2 tbsp oil with a fork. Add a little salt and pepper if you wish.

Put the sauce into a clean screw-top jar, label and store in a cool place.

Take the goose out of the fridge and leave it at cool room temperature for about 3 hours before cooking. Remove lumps of fat from inside the tail end of the bird. Wipe the bird inside and out with paper towels to check that it is perfectly dry. Peel the onion and quarter it. Quarter the orange without peeling it.

Put both onion and orange inside the bird and secure the gaps at both ends with skewers. Prick the skin of the goose all over with a fork, taking great care to angle it shallowly so it does not run deep into the flesh or you will encourage precious meat juices as well as fat to run out during cooking.

In a saucer, mix together 1 tsp each salt and freshly ground black pepper plus $\frac{1}{4}$ tsp each ground allspice and cinnamon. Sprinkle or rub this spicy mixture all over the skin of the bird. Weigh the bird and calculate the roasting time. (It is important to weigh it at this stage, not before, as the weight of the stuffing should be taken into consideration when making your calculation.)

Sit the goose, breast up, on a rack in a roasting tin and roast at 425°F (220°C), mark 7 for 20 minutes. Pour off the fat that has collected in the tin. Turn the bird breast down, reduce oven temperature to 350°F (180°C), mark 4 and roast for 1½ hours. Turn the bird breast up again. Baste it once with the fat that has collected in the tin, then pour the fat off and continue roasting.

About 15 minutes before your calculated time is up, look at the breast skin. If it is not as crisp as you would wish, dredge the breast with a little seasoned flour and complete roasting at a higher oven temperature—425°F (220°C), mark 7. Check that the goose is done by pricking the thigh meat: the juices that run from it should be clear, not pink.

To make the gravy, first pour all fat from the roasting tin. Add the stock and cider or wine and boil rapidly until reduced to a very small quantity of thin, richly flavoured gravy. Just a couple of spoonfuls per person is all that is needed.

Bring the goose to table on a very hot serving dish, surrounding the bird with Spiced and Stuffed Apples (right) and Rye Meatballs (page 132). Carve the goose very thinly and be sure that the dinner plates are piping hot. Spoon the gravy over the meat and hand around the sharply flavoured plum sauce in a sauceboat so that everyone can help themselves.

SERVES 8

SPICED AND STUFFED APPLES

This combination of dessert apples, spices and prunes provides a fine finishing touch for **Plum Perfect Goose.**

1 juicy crisp dessert apple per person
1 prune per person, soaked overnight in cider or cold tea
juice of 2 large juicy lemons
ground cinnamon and allspice
a little goose fat

Peel the apples thinly and cut out the cores. Squeeze the lemons, pouring juice into a large soup plate, add the apples and roll them around to moisten them with the juice to prevent discoloration.

Choose an ovenproof serving dish large enough to take the apples side by side. Grease it well with fat taken from the pan in which the goose is roasting, and put it in the oven for 10 minutes or so to become very hot. Put the apples into the ovenproof dish and roll them around to coat them with hot fat. Sprinkle a little ground cinnamon and allspice over them and drop one soaked, drained and chopped prune into the cavity of each.

Cover the dish with a dome of foil and bake on a shelf below the goose. The apples will need about 1 hour at 350°F (180°C), mark 4 to become hot and tender. Baste them several times as they cook and drain off the goose fat before serving. The cider in which the prunes were soaked can be saved and used to delicious advantage in making the goose gravy.

CHRYSANTHEMUM DUCK (PAGE 132)

RYE MEATBALLS

These meatballs are unusual. The flavouring of caraway and the use of rye bread make them particularly good for serving with a rich, fatty meat like goose.

1 lb (450 g) lean belly of pork (salt pork), boneless and de-rinded weight
1 onion
2 fat garlic cloves
caraway seeds and allspice
2 small slices rye bread
1 egg

Start making the meatballs a day ahead. Chop the onion finely and mince the pork.

Using some rendered down goose fat or a little oil, fry the onion gently for about 5 minutes to soften slightly, then add the minced pork and crushed garlic. Sprinkle on a scant ¾ tsp lightly crushed caraway seeds, a generous ¾ tsp allspice and some salt and pepper.

Stir to mix everything and fry gently for about 10 minutes. Meanwhile reduce the bread to crumbs. When the pork is ready, draw the pan away from the heat and stir in the breadcrumbs to sop up the fat and the juices. Turn the contents of the pan out on to a plate and leave until cold, then cover and refrigerate overnight.

Next day, work into the mixture with a fork as much lightly beaten egg as is needed to bind it to a good consistency. Shape into about 30 marble-sized balls.

To cook, put the meatballs side by side in a baking or roasting tin which has been generously greased with goose fat. Cover the tin with a dome of foil. Bake at 350°F (180°C), mark 4 on a shelf below the goose, allowing 30 minutes with the foil covering and 15 minutes without it. Shake the tin occasionally to roll and turn the meatballs as they bake to encourage even cooking.
MAKES 30 MEATBALLS

CHRYSANTHEMUM DUCK

With its glorious glaze and the bitter-sweet fragrance of the accompanying salad, this makes a sensational alternative to classic crispy roast duck. No problems about carving—duck joints are used. Just add or subtract to cater for larger or smaller parties.

6 large duck joints
fresh root ginger
5 small thin-skinned oranges
a little runny honey and soy sauce
1–2 large chrysanthemums, preferably tawny gold
watercress or chicory (endive)
a few unsalted cashew nuts, toasted under the grill (broiler)

Remove any lumps of excess fat from the duck joints, and prick the skin all over with a fork, angling it carefully to avoid piercing deep into the flesh or precious meat juices as well as fat will run out during cooking. Peel and chop very finely indeed 2 generous tbsp fresh root ginger.

Lay the duck joints in a dish and rub them all over with the ginger and a good grinding of pepper, but no salt. Pour on 2 tbsp juice freshly squeezed from one orange. Turn the meat several times to moisten it all over. Cover and set aside in a cool place for several hours, preferable overnight, so the duck absorbs some of the flavours.

Drain the marinade from the duck and scrape off the ginger. Reserve this and the marinade liquid. Put the duck joints, skin side up, on to a rack in a baking dish or roasting tin and roast in an oven heated to 400°F (200°C), mark 6 for 45 minutes. (If the duck joints are very large and your oven is quite small you may need to use two dishes and two racks—and swap oven positions half-way through cooking.)

Stand the honey jar in a bowl of hot water for 10 minutes so that the honey becomes runny enough to measure easily. Mix 2 tbsp of the honey with the orange and ginger marinade mixture, then stir in 2 tsp soy sauce plus a pinch of salt to make an aromatic glaze.

Pour off the duck fat that has collected in the roasting tin—save it for frying. Brush the glaze all over the flesh and skin of the duck and continue roasting, still with skin side up and still on the rack, for another 20 minutes. Baste once during this time, making sure that all the little pieces of ginger adhere to the duck skin. By the end of the cooking time the meat should be well-cooked yet succulent and the skin should be burnished to a rich mahogany-coloured glaze. If the duck looks in danger of burning, cover the dish with a dome of foil. More probably it will only be necessary to cover only the wing tips or drumsticks—the parts which are most prone to burning.

To make the accompanying salad, first peel 3–4 small thin-skinned oranges. Use a very sharp knife and be ruthless about cutting away every trace of the bitter white pith. Slice the oranges across into thin rounds, sprinkle them with a little pepper, a scrunch of sea-salt and a drizzle of oil. Arrange them prettily in a shallow dish. Add a few nuts if you wish and a scant handful of chicory leaves or watercress sprigs, but bear in mind that the salad should be composed mainly of orange and chrysanthemum. Immediately before serving, sprinkle the salad with another spoonful of oil and a squeeze of orange, then quickly pile the fresh chrysanthemum petals on top. The slightly bitter fragrance of the flowers complements the rich glazed duck beautifully. Huge tawny gold blooms look most dramatic: simply pull the petals from the flower heads, tugging them gently, a small handful at a time, so they do not become bruised or spoiled.

SERVES 6

FORESTER'S PHEASANT

Choose birds with undamaged breast skin for this dish or the stuffing will ooze out. If the tear is very small the flow can be stemmed by bandaging with bacon. Show off the richly sauced birds to full advantage with perfectly plain accompaniments such as boiled noodles and peppery watercress.

brace of pheasant
¼ lb (125 g) cream cheese or low-fat soft cheese
2 tbsp freshly grated Parmesan cheese
4 tbsp chopped fresh parsley
1½ tsp dried tarragon
1 lb/8 cups (450 g) mushrooms (small cap or oyster mushrooms)
giblet stock and unsalted butter
1 finely chopped garlic clove
5 tbsp Marsala
½ pint/1¼ cups (275 ml) double (heavy) cream

Make the stuffing by mashing the Parmesan into the soft cheese, together with the herbs and plenty of salt and pepper.

Put your fingers under the neck-skin of one of the birds and gently and gradually ease the skin away from the breast. Push half of the stuffing gently into place, spreading it evenly all over the flesh of the breast, then tuck the loose end flap of the neck skin under the bird and secure with a small wooden skewer. Prepare the second pheasant in the same way.

Brown the birds all over in 1½ oz/3 tbsp (40 g) unsalted butter. Take great care when browning the breast area. Season the pheasants and arrange them breast down in a flameproof casserole. Lay a sheet of buttered greaseproof paper directly on top of the birds and cover with a well fitting lid. Pot roast at 400°F (200°C), mark 6 until tender and cooked—about 45 minutes.

Transfer the birds to a warmed dish and let them rest. Add the well flavoured giblet stock to the buttery pheasant juices in the casserole and fast-boil until the mixture is reduced to scant ½ pint/1¼ cups (300 ml) very savoury gravy. Pour the gravy into a jug and reserve.

Carve the birds, cutting from each 4 slices of breast, 2 drumsticks and 2 thigh pieces. Put the meat on to a serving dish, cover and keep hot.

Warm a 12 inch (30 cm) frying pan and melt ½ oz/1 tbsp (15 g) butter in it. Add the mushrooms —thickly sliced if they are cap mushrooms, cut into thin strips if oyster mushrooms—and the garlic.

Cover the pan with a large plate or a piece of foil and cook over very low heat for 4 minutes, just shaking the pan occasionally. Remove the covering, increase heat to moderate, and fry, stirring and turning the mushrooms frequently, for a further 3 minutes or so to drive off the liquid exuded and to concentrate the flavour of the mushrooms deliciously.

Pour the gravy and the Marsala into the frying pan and leave to cook at a fierce bubble for a couple of minutes. Add the cream and let the mixture bubble over more moderate heat, just stirring occasionally, for about 5 minutes until the liquids are smoothly blended and reduced to a rich syrupy sauce. Season well with plenty of pepper, some salt and perhaps a squeeze of lemon.

Pour the sauce over the pheasants, cover and leave in a low oven for 10 minutes or so before serving. Serve with plenty of plain boiled noodles— spinach noodles perhaps—or lots of good bread and an undressed watercress salad to mop up the exquisite sauce.

SERVES 6–8

PARTRIDGE IN THE VINE

Vine leaves have a long and honourable history in the English kitchen. Tudor and Stuart cooks stewed them with fruit, and Hannah Glasse recommended vine-leaf fritters, but vine leaves were most often used—as here—to wrap and seal in the juices of delicately flavoured meats during cooking. The use of grapes and grape juice is a natural extension of the gentle fruity theme and nicely complements the subtle taste of partridge.

4 plump young partridge

2 oz/½ stick (50 g) butter and a little olive oil

4 large rashers (slices) streaky bacon

1 or 2 vine leaves per bird, or cabbage leaves if vine leaves are unobtainable

4–8 large thick rounds of bread

1–2 bunches of watercress

6 fl oz/¾ cup (175 ml) unsweetened white grape juice

3 oz/generous ½ cup (75 g) white grapes per person, preferably muscatel

If using fresh vine leaves, make them pliable by blanching. Drop them into a pan of fast-boiling water; cook for 1–1½ minutes, drain well and pat dry with kitchen paper towels. If using brined vine leaves, soak, rinse and dry them carefully following instructions on the packet or tin. Cabbage leaves may not be as romantic but they are a good and practical alternative. Choose the large, outer leaves of a firm green-leafed cabbage such as savoy, and blanch them, as described for fresh vine leaves, to make them easier to use for wrapping.

Put a hazelnut-sized knob of well seasoned butter into the body cavity of each bird and rub the skin all over with salt and freshly ground black pepper. Cut the bacon rashers in half if long. Cover the breasts of the birds with the bacon, then encase each bird completely in a neat wrapping of leaves and tie securely with string.

To prepare the grapes it is necessary only to halve and seed them. I have tried this recipe using grapes which have been peeled as well as halved and seeded and concluded that the extra effort involved was not justified—unless the grapes have unusually coarse thick skins.

Flute the rounds of bread prettily, fry them lightly in best-quality olive oil, drain well and keep them hot.

To cook the partridge, first lay the birds breast down on a rack in a roasting tin. Melt the remaining butter and pout it over them. Roast at 425°F (220°C), mark 7 for 15 minutes. Baste the birds thoroughly with the buttery pan juices, turn them breast up and roast for 15 minutes more.

Then unparcel the birds, removing vine leaves and bacon wrappings. Baste the birds well with the pan juices and continue roasting for a further 5–6 minutes, breast up, until the skin is pale golden brown. Tilt the birds to let the juices run from the body cavities back into the roasting pan.

Transfer the birds on to a warmed serving dish, placing each one on a round of hot fried bread (or halve the birds first if serving one between two people) and put to rest in a warm place for 15 minutes or so before serving.

Skim some of the fat from the roasting pan. Add the grapes and the grape juice to the pan and shake to swirl and moisten the grapes. Put the pan into the switched-off oven (or place it directly over a very low flame) for a few minutes to warm and slightly soften the fruit. Lift the grapes out of the pan with a slotted spoon, pile them round the birds and garnish with a big clump of watercress. Season the grape-juice gravy remaining in the pan with salt and pepper to taste, and transfer to a warmed sauce boat. A few game chips or potato sticks are the only other accompaniment that is necessary.

SERVES 4–8

GUINEA-FOWL WITH POMEGRANATES

Raspberry vinegar (page 55), a traditional product of the English country kitchen, is crucial to the aromatic effect of this delectably elegant dish, which is an admirable choice for a small celebration. I find the most effective way to extract the juice of a pomegranate is to tip the garnet-coloured seeds into a piece of butter-muslin, twist the cloth tightly and squeeze with your hands.

1 guinea-fowl, or poulet noir
2 pomegranates
1 orange and lots of watercress
2 oz (50 g) cream cheese, curd cheese or low-fat
   soft cheese
6–8 juniper berries
clarified or unsalted butter
¼ pint/⅔ cup (150 ml) reduced giblet stock
2 tbsp raspberry vinegar
6 oz/1 cup (175 g) brown rice
2½ oz/⅓ cup (40 g) split or flaked almonds, well toasted

Several hours before cooking, crush the juniper berries and finely grate the zest of the orange. Mix together. Mash half this mixture into the cream cheese and season with salt and pepper.

Slip your fingers under the flap of neck skin and gently ease the breast skin from the flesh of the fowl. Gently push and spread the cream cheese mixture into the pocket you have formed, then secure the flap of neck skin under the bird with a few stitches or a small skewer. Put the other half of the orange zest and juniper mixture into the body cavity of the bird together with a good seasoning of salt and pepper. Pour the juice of the orange over the bird and set it aside in a cool place for at least 1 hour.

When ready to cook, drain off the orange juice and dry the bird gently. Brown it all over in a little very hot butter—take care of the breast area. Transfer it to an oval flameproof casserole which will just hold it snugly. Season with salt and pepper, place a sheet of lightly buttered greaseproof paper over the breast and cover with a well fitting lid.

Pot-roast in the oven at 400°F (200°C), mark 6 until the meat is cooked through, succulent and tender—35 minutes or so for guinea-fowl, probably nearer 1 hour for poulet noir. Check that it is done by piercing the thickest part of the thigh: the juices that run from it should be clear, not pink.

While the bird is pot-roasting, cook the rice in double its volume of liquid—salted water plus 1 tbsp raspberry vinegar. Cut both pomegranates in half. Extract the juice from one of the fruits, strain

it, mix it with the well flavoured giblet stock and 1 tbsp raspberry vinegar and set aside for making the gravy.

Pick the beautiful garnet-coloured seeds out of the other pomegranate, carefully discarding all the creamy yellow strands of pith. Gently mix the seeds with the well-toasted almonds and season generously with salt and pepper. Fold in the cooked rice when it is ready.

Carefully lift the pot-roast guinea-fowl out of the casserole and let it rest in a warm place for at least 10 minutes before carving or jointing. Add the prepared gravy liquid to the buttery juices remaining in the casserole. Let the mixture bubble up and boil rapidly until blended to make a rich, slightly sharp and aromatic gravy.

Joint or carve the bird for serving and garnish it with generous clumps of watercress (no other green vegetable is necessary). Pass round separately the pomegranate and almond rice and the gravy. The aromatic gravy is intended to moisten the watercress and the rice as well as the poultry.

SERVES 3–4

COOK'S NOTEBOOK

When I was a girl old wives used to say that the way to a man's heart was through his stomach. True maybe, but don't forget that the way to a man's heart attack may also be thought his stomach. It's not a pretty thought, I admit, but it is salutary to remind ourselves of the facts occasionally.

The cook is ultimately responsible for what is eaten at her table. The well-being of the family, and to some extent of friends, depends on what foods she serves—and, above all else perhaps—on how *much* she serves. The cook wields much more power than most of us care to acknowledge. She is the corner-stone in the whole process of the giving and taking of foods, a process of sharing which touches a fundamental core in all of us. Food is more than nutrition. Subconsciously it is tightly intertwined with our feelings about love, friendship and caring. Sharing food strengthens bonds and most of us are reluctant to refuse, because refusal seems tantamount to rejecting the person who has prepared and offered the food.

We have all had the experience of being invited to a meal in someone else's house where we have been plied, in the nicest possible way, with too much food. We've felt cornered but we've smiled and eaten it all up, not because we really needed or wanted it but for the sake of good manners, in order to avoid offending the generous provider.

You might think it would be easier to say no at home, but in many ways the constraints are much greater within the family context because the stakes are higher. The need to love and to be loved is strong and nobody enjoys running the risk of rejecting or being rejected by those closest to them. When a wife offers her husband or children more than she believes is good for them, she may be deliberately over-providing for fear of appearing mean and unloving. Similarly, a husband or children may tuck into much more than they really want simply not to seem ungrateful.

It's up to the cook to make the first move for the better: prepare sensible quantities, not enough to feed an army; never press food on others; and let them make up their own minds about when they've had enough—unless they show signs of greediness. The cook must not take offence if small helpings are asked for, nor interpret lack of requests for second helpings as unspoken criticism of her cooking.

When left to our own devices most of us are quite modest eaters. We like good food, carefully chosen and cooked, in moderate quantities rather than massive blow-outs, and we eat fairly sensibly in the normal course of events.

One of the main dangers of not eating wisely occurs when entertaining. Then the cook seems to develop a sudden urge to be super-generous (I am putting it politely), lashing out with many more courses than usual and often adopting a much more elaborate and rich style of cooking. The aim is to give guests a great welcome. In my experience it is liable to give them indigestion.

Even when party menus are planned with sensible restraint, we can succumb to silly temptations at the 11th hour. I am guilty of convincing myself in the middle of a shopping expedition that I ought to buy some cheese too "just in case". And at Christmas, when the shops will be shut for several days, it is easy to persuade ourselves that we ought to stock up with extra-large quantities of everything and some supplementary goodies as well "just in case". Oh fatal phrase "just in case", password to the cook's undoing.

When I think of scenes of over-eating, I can't help remembering the method of obtaining *foie gras* in France by force-feeding the geese. The birds are literally spoon-fed and their poor throats are massaged to help down the enormous quantities of food. If there is even the smallest element of this in our approach to feeding our family and friends we had best beware!

Before we next cajole the baby into finishing his bottle, before we press someone to second helpings, before we say "let's finish this up, there's hardly enough to be worth saving for another meal", before we start planning a showoff party menu, let's stop and think. Who are we trying to please? Do they really want or need so much or will they eat it up just to please the cook? This is not to suggest that some people are not inherently greedy—they are—but the cook can fan the flames of that greed and make it into a real problem. (Or she can quietly and gently help to damp it down.) We are creatures of habit. Once used to big meals, we need them regularly to satisfy us—and the problem just grows and grows.

QUAILS ON CUSHIONS

All the preparations for this recipe can be done well ahead leaving you only to pop the birds into the oven shortly before you plan to serve them. Quails are quick to cook, they need no basting and can be kept hot for 20–30 minutes without drying out or otherwise spoiling—a trio of virtues which will endear them to the hostess.

8 quail
¼ lb/2 cups (125 g) mushrooms
½ lb (225 g) chicken livers
1½ tbsp brandy
a little garlic and butter
8 slices white bread
6 small thin-skinned oranges
coriander and cumin seeds
half very small onion
a little olive oil and a few small black olives

First make the stuffing. Chop all the mushrooms and half the chicken livers very finely. Sauté the mushrooms in a very small nugget of butter for just 2–3 minutes to drive off some of their juices. Add the prepared chicken livers and continue frying a little longer. Tip the mixture into a soup plate, season it with salt, pepper and a little garlic. Let it become cold, then crush with a fork until it is quite smooth.

Next make the pâté-type mixture to spread on the toasts (the cushions) on which the quails will be served. Cut the remaining chicken livers into big pieces. Sauté them in a little butter for 2–3 minutes until crusty and brown on the outside but still tender and pink within. Flame them with the brandy, then crush them into the buttery pan juices. Season with salt and set aside to become cold.

To prepare the quails for cooking, first sit them breast up on a work surface. Press the palm of your hand down lightly on the breast of each bird to flatten it a little. Insert your fingers under the neck skin and loosen the skin from the breast to make a pocket for the stuffing.

Push in the stuffing, gently and neatly. Then make a slit through the tail-end of the breast, cross the birds' legs and tuck the ends through the slit. This will give the bird a plumper, neater appearance. Prepare the other quails in the same way.

To make the spicy salad—an integral part of the recipe—first squeeze the juice from half an orange into a pretty glass dish. Peel the rest of the oranges, ruthlessly removing all traces of bitter white pith. Slice the flesh thinly and put it into the bowl. Scatter with raw onion sliced wafer thin, and some miniature Provençal black olives—the sort that are no larger than hazelnut kernels and which taste beautifully sweet. Add a generous drizzle of fruity olive oil, cover and set aside.

Toast the bread and cut into rounds just large enough to take the quails. Spread the toasts with the cold chicken-liver mixture and put them side by side in a shallow lightly greased baking dish. Sit a bird on each, brush the skins of the birds with a little olive oil and sprinkle with salt and pepper.

To cook, roast the quail on their cushions at 400°F (200°C), mark 6 for 25–30 minutes until they are cooked through and tender. Cover the dish and put to rest in a warm place for at least 10 minutes.

Serve accompanied only by the salad, which should, at the last moment, be sprinkled with a scrunch of sea-salt and some coriander and cumin seeds (toasted and lightly bruised to heighten their aroma). It is of course impossible to tackle such a small bird with knife and fork only. Fingers are the order of the day and fingerbowls will be needed.
SERVES 4–8

INDEX